Which One Am I?

12 Extraordinary People, Like You!

LARRY J. SNYDER

IRONTWINE
—— P R E S S ——

Which One Am I?

12 Extraordinary People, Like You!

LARRY J. SNYDER

www.WhichOne.Life

Published by Iron Twine Press
www.IronTwinePress.com

Cover and book design by Sonja L. Gerard

Back cover photo by Larry J. Snyder

The headshot photos within this book were provided by the indivduals in the profiles.

Printed in the United States of America.
Paperbound edition of this book originally printed by:
Quality Press, 222 South Orcas Street, Seattle, Washington 98108
www.QualityPress.com

ISBN 978-0-9970600-7-2 (pb)

10 9 8 7 6 5 4 3 2 1

To the most extraordinary woman in the world:

my mom, Jean.

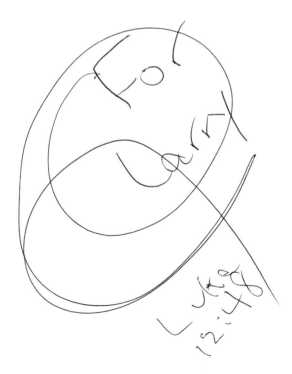

Also by Larry J. Snyder

Miracles in Montanare: Ten Years in Tuscany

CONTENTS

FOREWORD

BY **MARGARET LARSON**

You meet people from time to time who've taken life experience and turned it into a life's work. Maybe they're receiving an award or being featured in a newspaper. But without saying a word, they invite us to ask ourselves, "could I do that? What did it take for them to envision a way to make a difference?"

In Larry Snyder's moving book, we hear from people who've done extraordinary things, and it's tempting to think that what they've accomplished is beyond our reach. After all, we most often read about people like Bill Gates working on inoculating children around the world, Bono spearheading humanitarian responses, or Matt Damon trying to bring clean water to everyone. It all seems so huge.

But then I think about the international civil servant, Robert Muller, who—among other things—created the World Food Programme at the United Nations, now the largest humanitarian organization working on eliminating hunger in the history of mankind. I heard Mr. Muller speak at the University of Washington, where he told the audience about his upbringing in Alsace-Lorraine, witnessing the horrors of World War II, surviving as a refugee, even undertaking death-defying activities as a member of the French Resistance.

But when it came time for the Q & A with the audience, this remarkably good-humored servant of humanity, who had lived such a big life, showed a decidedly pragmatic streak. After listening to an audience member list out the many disasters and conflicts around the world and express his worry about the many things that seemed totally beyond his capacity to affect, Mr. Muller asked a simple question: "Did you pick up the trash on your way to work today? If not, start there. You'll feel better." And then he chuckled, not from any sort of derision, but as a way to encourage us all to know, really know, that we can always affect our surroundings, our neighbors, our world. Even if we start small, maybe *especially* if we start small, we can discover the power of our own actions.

Robert Muller's small and practical point, even after all that he'd created in his truly amazing life, has stuck with me ever since. His life, and the lives of the people you'll read about in this book, are awe-inspiring. But the ingredients that made their life's work possible are the same ingredients that you and I are made of.

One of Larry's subjects, and a friend of mine, is Cindy Nofziger. I first met her when she earned the 2012 Jefferson Award in Washington state, a sort of "Nobel Prize" for public service. She was thoroughly humble about the honor bestowed upon her and seemed almost bemused to be in the company of the other award winners. Not long before, Cindy had been a physical therapist for Seattle Public Schools, with no intentions of starting a charitable organization.

But in 2004, when she returned to Sierra Leone where she had served a stint in the Peace Corps in the 1980s, she witnessed the ravages of the civil war there. A friend asked her for help in rebuilding a single school. Simple as that. And thus began an organic set of activities that unfolded over months and years, and resulted in the construction of twelve new schools by the time Cindy received the Jefferson award. By then, her nonprofit Schools for Salone was thoroughly established, winning praise and support from former Peace Corps workers, international athletes, civic leaders, and so many others.

At the time of this writing, Schools for Salone has constructed 22 schools and three libraries (with more on the way), trained 150 teachers, reached nearly 7,000 students, created several hygiene stations, and been instrumental in rebuilding communities after the Ebola epidemic.

Cindy would tell you that she is not extraordinary. She would tell you that Sierra Leone and its people are the ones who should be credited. And for certain, the Schools for Salone team in Sierra Leone has worked tirelessly and selflessly to make a difference. I guess, in the end, I would say that Cindy and her team, both in the U.S. and Sierra Leone, have done extraordinary things by simply following the ordinary and very decent instincts of a caring person.

And isn't the takeaway that we know, we *feel*, what's

right? We all know that life feels best when we extend a hand to others. It is not beyond us or too big for us. Larry's stories help us drink that notion in. He has chosen individual human beings to feature but the lessons apply to all of us, every single one of us, all the time. The stories in this remarkable book call out to us, encouraging us to look inside and to grab the moment. The magic and beauty of bringing people together and making a difference in our world right this very minute, is *always* within our reach.

I've long admired Margaret for her work as a journalist sharing stories in front of the camera from all over the world. For 30 years, Margaret has helped audiences really understand what's occurring in some of the most impoverished places on earth. In less challenging environments, Margaret shares the stories of extraordinary people on KING 5 TV's *New Day Northwest*. Her philanthropy and community engagement inspires me to always be looking for new ways to serve others.
~ L. S.

MARGARET LARSON

Which One Am I?

12 Extraordinary People, Like You!

Hardworking
Patient · Intuitive
Compassionate
Open-minded

WAYNE SLATER

For the past five years, I've admired how Mr. Wayne enthusiastically keeps a room of Saturday morning piano students and their parents excited about making music, my daughter included. He's an extraordinary music teacher. ~ L. S.

For the past three decades, Mr. Wayne Slater has taught piano, organ, music theory and composition. Receiving a Fulbright Scholarship for post-graduate studies at the Conservatory of music in Cologne, Germany, he's also performed numerous recitals throughout the U.S. and Europe. As a music teacher, middle C on the keyboard is Wayne Slater's favorite, and his relationship to every aspiring student and hopeful parent starts with this first white key. Once the mastery of middle C is complete, two black keys, and years worth of practice with a familiar weekly homework sheet follow.

Mr. Wayne, as he is known to his students, does much more than teach kids how to play the piano. He will tell you with a smile that he only teaches music on the days that end with Y and admit he's not sure if he's working seven days a week or just living his life. His patient, witty, and engaging methodology keeps even the youngest kids at attention during their weekly one-hour class. He's following the work ethic of a Kansas farmer.

Mr. Wayne's 92-year-old father, Russell, worked exhaustive hours to support his dedicated wife and six children. In addition to farming his own land and the acreage of dozens of others, he picked up part-time work in a factory, as a postman, and a telephone lineman, setting an example for his son that Mr. Wayne has followed and modeled to his own three children and students.

Keeping Wayne's childhood house of eight moving forward took a Super Mom. June Slater, Wayne's mother, was that and much more. She drove trucks, tore down a chicken coop, grew beautiful flowers and baked bread; all of these while singing a song. Life in the Slater's Midwest farm household was never short on solid advice for how to live. June gave Wayne the gift of knowing a "Pocket Day." When the temperature is just right, it's not too windy and the day is perfect in every way, one can pocket that day and pull it out later to improve on another that isn't going in your favor. Today, Mr. Wayne follows his mom's counsel to look for beauty in the nooks and crannies of the world. Not a day passes by that he's not studying obscure places most people overlook.

When he was just four years old, one of the places he found that brought him lasting joy was the keys of a player piano that his parents brought home. Even though the tight household budget could not afford it, this first set of 88 keys was, for Wayne, the catalyst to a lifetime of music performance and impassioned teaching.

MR. WAYNE'S FAVORITE QUOTES

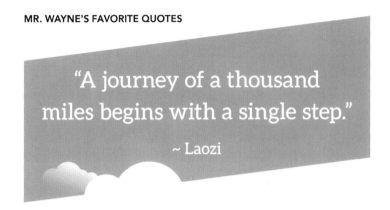

"A journey of a thousand miles begins with a single step."

~ Laozi

At ten years old, Mr. Wayne sat behind the wheel of a combine, and he drove his first load of wheat to the grain elevator at twelve. Now, each morning, as he walks through the door at his Pied Piper Music Studio, a bit of that Kansas work ethic enters too. Like faming in the Midwest, running a nonstop music education program is an all-hands-on-deck operation. Lucky for Mr. Wayne, his wife of 37 years, Diane, is as passionate about middle C as he is. Between their four hands, the day-to-day operation of Pied Piper has brought the joy of music into thousands of Redmond, Washington homes since 1988.

As each student settles in front of the piano and rests his or her fingers on the keys, Mr. Wayne summons his upbringing as a farmer. His parents gifted him with many important values, none greater than acknowledging that everyone has potential. He waters that seed and doesn't give up because he knows the fruits of his labor are not immediate. With three decades of moving all ages of kids through the progression of piano study, Mr. Wayne never knows when all that practice at home will deliver the next musician like him. But he knows that, with the right nurturing, such a delivery is possible.

One of the many benefits parents receive having their kids in Mr. Wayne's care is being able to sit behind them during class. Such an arrangement is unusual in most youth classrooms, where often the teacher, student or both can feel the presence of a parent is an imposition. But Mr. Wayne attributes achievement to a three-way relationship between a willing child, an engaged parent, and a dynamic teacher.

Mr. Wayne's own potential was realized early through the example of education and the attention of caring teachers. Both June and Russell were voracious readers. Mr. Wayne knows his parents' brilliant minds are due, in large part, to always having had a book at hand. In high school, Wayne had the good fortune of studying under the new band director, Mr. Moots. Fresh from earning his bachelor's degree and at work on his Master's degree in trumpet performance, Mr. Moots saw something extraordinary in Wayne. Wayne took every opportunity to spend as much time as possible being guided by his new mentor. Not long into their friendship, Mr. Moots shared his observation that, based on his obvious love of music and his drive to learn, Mr. Wayne should spend his college days studying music.

Wayne followed that advice and headed for Wichita State University. Upon entering college there, Mr. Wayne found himself surrounded by others that shared his passion for piano and the study of music theory. An important friendship formed with several other students, including Blair Penney. Both Mr. Wayne and Blair entered the program with an undefined professional path but shared a belief that if they each worked hard, supported one another and had fun along the way, things would all work out. At that awkward crossroads of adolescence and adulthood, when it is so common to be wrestling with one's self concept and need to fit in, Blair showed Mr. Wayne a road less traveled. While everyone around them was competing for social status using traditional methods, Blair cultivated his place through kindness, being inspiring to others, and looking for ways to lend a hand to students needing extra assistance. Mr. Wayne found accepting himself and others was a source of calm and gave him a deeper enthusiasm for school. To this day, he recognizes Blair's influence in his own approach to his students.

At Wichita State it was the guidance of another valued teacher that kept Wayne on track, though this guidance was not as easy to follow as Mr. Moot's had been. Wayne's organ professor, Mr. Robert Town, noticed Wayne was spending what he felt was far too much time with a certain girl. The professor believed some of that time should be spent at the keys instead. His basic message to Wayne was: you simply will never reach your potential if you don't discover it. Prior to performance await hours and days of mastering basic skills. The professor wanted Wayne to discover amazement in his own ability.

MR. WAYNE'S FAVORITE QUOTES

"To experience harmony, one must first experience discord."

~ Confucius

Reluctantly Wayne took his teacher's counsel about the girl and invested those romantic hours at the organ instead. That guidance alone started an appreciation for unending practice, which led to a Fulbright Scholarship, a life-defining educational opportunity. During his study abroad in Germany on the Fulbright, a violin player from Seattle caught Wayne's eye. Her name was Diane and she began talking about the benefits of a life together in Seattle, a land unknown to Mr. Wayne.

Few couples can say they truly make beautiful music together. In addition to helping kids get started on piano, Diane is a sought-after flute instructor. With studio doors facing each other, Mr. Wayne and Diane celebrate a lot of the same victories and occasionally endure a few of the defeats a family business can deliver. Although there is that adage "opposites attract," much of what has made this partnership of family and business grow are the similarities between Diane and Mr. Wayne. Admitting that he married up and that most of everything good in his life came of Diane's doing, Mr. Wayne believes 37 years of marriage is easy, so long as you find the right person.

The love of teaching music at Mr. Wayne's house did not end with Wayne and Diane. Should a need arise, Mr. Wayne's family has all the pieces for a true house band. With first daughter, Stephanie, on piano and flute, second daughter, Emily, playing piano and flute, as well as son, Ethan, on percussion, Mr. Wayne's home is rarely without the sound of high quality music when other family comes to visit. With the fourth grandchild just around the corner, the next generation has a good chance of being in love with music too. Pied Piper has been the beneficiary of Mr. Wayne's offspring in teaching roles as well. Both Stephanie and Ethan have sat in the teacher's seat imparting the week's lesson in the same spirit as their parents. Following their entrepreneurial mother and father, Stephanie and Emily recently founded STEM Floral Design using the first two letters of their respective birth names as a company identifier. Mr. Wayne and Diane have great pride in how the family values have showed up in their children, specifically in the size of their hearts, how they assume their roles in being socially responsible, and in their strong sense of justice.

MR. WAYNE'S FAVORITE QUOTES

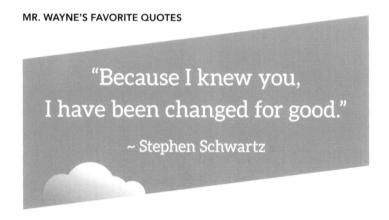

"Because I knew you,
I have been changed for good."
~ Stephen Schwartz

Faith has also played an important role in Mr. Wayne's personal and professional life. Though he would not describe himself as a religious man, he has spent plenty of time amongst the pews. He started with the piano, and then the organ, in his small Kansas church. Mr. Wayne's current church role is in a room much bigger. As the church organist for the past three decades at Bellevue Presbyterian, Mr. Wayne's Sunday congregation is many times the size of the crowd back home. As Mr. Wayne looks back, he cannot remember a time that he hasn't had a steady role behind the keys on Sunday, but for Mr. Wayne faith isn't just about church. Investing energy and time into a child at Pied Piper takes faith. Growing a fantastic garden takes faith. Mr. Wayne appreciates what the Creator has placed in his hands. He loves nature and has an appreciation for being able to see in color, hear water in a brook, and taste bacon. Having a mind that stores all his best thoughts only adds to his gratitude for life.

Like the Kansas farmer, a bit of Mr. Moots and Mr. Town follow Mr. Wayne through the door every day at Pied Piper. After an hour with Mr. Wayne, each student gets to take a little of them home. Many others, near and far, have had a say in how this son of a Kansas farmer would build an accomplished business, a marriage with staying power, and three productive children. From all these ingredients, Mr. Wayne has found three words he believes are a recipe for a happy and worthwhile life: Read, Listen, and Observe.

A source of continued drive and motivation for Mr. Wayne walks though his studio door at the beginning of each September. Most are returning students after a summer break, but some will sit behind one of the 16 Yamaha keyboards for the first time. This chance to bring music into the lives and homes of a new group of fresh minds keeps Mr. Wayne inspired. With parents seated hopefully behind them, Mr. Wayne issues the eager student a brand-new *Harmony Road Music Course* book, has them find the power button, and has them place their right index finger on middle C.

WAYNE SLATER

Inspiring
Assiduous · Productive
Responsive
Collaborative

CINDY NOFZIGER

My heart was reshaped after traveling to West Africa with Cindy in 2016. There are nearly 7,000 educated children in Sierra Leone (West Africa) because Cindy made the extraordinary decision to help a friend build a single village school there in 2005. Today, there are almost two dozen schools and counting. ~ L. S.

Maforeka, a tribal village of 800 in north central Sierra Leone (West Africa) is welcoming a friendly visitor. This isn't her first visit. In fact, Cindy Nofziger, founder of Seattle-based Schools for Salone, has lost count how many times she's set foot on the make-shift playground in front of the primary school that she and her generous stateside friends helped build. "*Seen dee*" is what the children scream when they see her delegation pull in. These school children, and those of 23 other villages throughout this tiny coastal African nation, have what most other rural villages can only dream of. They have schools, which provide an educated alternative beyond subsistence farming. It's a fundamental shift in their human experience, not just for the school children but for the entire village.

Cindy's love and passion for Africa wasn't intentional.

Through the loss of her father to cancer when she was 21 and being raped at gun point in an upscale part of Washington, D.C., Cindy felt lost and alone. From the time she was young, growing up in the small Mennonite village of Goshen, Indiana, Cindy always had thoughts of different cultures in faraway places. In her early twenties, Cindy's path of discovery aligned with a friend who had served with the Peace Corps in Nepal. Cindy applied to this organization which was created during the John F. Kennedy administration. With little influence over where she'd be stationed, Cindy was accepted to use her new Physical Therapy Master's Degree in Sierra Leone, a country she'd never heard of. Realizing she'd most likely never find her way there again, she took the three-year assignment.

Cindy came to realize that through a sense of purpose and a new family made of friends, the Peace Corps saved her life. Her specific assignment was at a small leprosy hospital in Masanga, a rural village in eastern Sierra Leone. During those formidable days of treating patients with differing ailments, including leprosy, several key people would become Cindy's inner circle. One of them was Sierra Leonean, and fellow physical therapist, John Sesay. Another important local and would-be confidant was Joseph Lemin. Both men helped Cindy impact the hospital patients and those needing help in the outlying villages. A third key member of the group was fellow American, Robin, who was responsible for the original request to bring a physical therapist to Masanga. She, too, would become a member of

Cindy's chosen family in Sierra Leone. Alongside Joseph, Robin also spent her Peace Corps days both in the Masanga hospital and out in the neighboring villages implementing community health projects.

Concluding her days in West Africa, Cindy moved back to the Washington, D.C. area where she would eventually regroup with Peace Corps friends, including Robin. The allure and textured experience of working abroad made Cindy seek out new opportunities in faraway places. Her next professional calling would be teaching physical therapy in Kathmandu, Nepal, followed by Uganda and Zanzibar. Returning to the east coast of the U.S. no longer had the appeal it did before. Several Peace Corps friends had headed west to Seattle, so that would be Cindy's next outpost. Buying her first home upon arrival to Seattle meant she was done traveling the world, at least for a little while. This is the same north Seattle home where Cindy lives today.

A short few years later, after an introduction by her trusted friend Peggy, who had walked side by side through some of Cindy's toughest days, including the death of her father, Cindy met and married Dr. Ken Lans. Peggy was also a rape survivor and an influential force in Cindy's life. The two women supported each other at every level. When Cindy learned she was expecting, Peggy was her pregnancy coach and eventually a doula when Michael was born. Unfortunately, Peggy fell ill and died just before Michael's first birthday. Today, Cindy still maintains a close relationship with the four children and spouse Peggy left behind. She also keeps tight communication with all her fellow Sierra Leone Peace Corps friends. In 2004, she joined a reunion in Freetown, the capital city of Sierra Leone. For the first time in a decade, Cindy returned to West Africa.

CINDY'S FAVORITE QUOTES

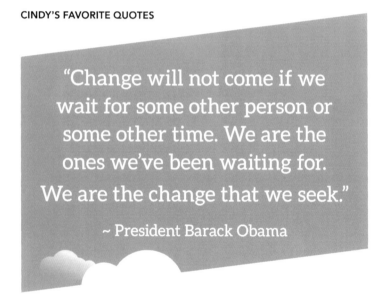

"Change will not come if we wait for some other person or some other time. We are the ones we've been waiting for. We are the change that we seek."

~ President Barack Obama

It was just two years after the civil war and Cindy was a bit apprehensive, but she knew it would be a worthwhile adventure. After an eventful flight across the Atlantic including a prolonged wait in Ghana, Cindy spotted Joseph and his memorable smile. Cindy nearly jumped into his arms as they met for the first time since their days in Masanga at the leprosy hospital. As an added surprise, John Sesay had made the long trip from Maforeka and was waiting when Cindy arrived at Joseph's guest house. He, too, was overjoyed. In the coming days, Cindy traveled to Masanga. Her emotions overcame her when she witnessed the destruction of the ten-year civil war that had spared only a few of the buildings she remembered so vividly from her time there. During her visit, John asked Cindy a question she is still answering more than a dozen years later: could Cindy find a way to help rebuild the primary school in Maforeka that was destroyed during the war? John gave her a handful of drawings from the school children in Maforeka. Those drawings became note cards that Cindy packaged and sold in the U.S. to fund the rebuilding of John's village school. The new Maforeka village school opened in 2005.

Cindy exemplifies the African proverb, "I am because we are," with a quiet, pervasive warmth that permeates any room she enters. Stateside, her enthusiasm for building schools grew through her association with Friends of Sierra Leone. Several of those with whom she served had their own village school projects underway. One of them was Bob Heavner, who was fundraising to build a school in Mambolo, where he had served during his Peace Corps days. During that same period, Cindy would continue to develop supporters for Joseph's organization, Masanga Children's Fund, which would go on to change its name to Programme for Children. At the same time, Cindy's marriage to Ken was suffering. Eventually their heated arguments strained the relationship to the point of no return and Cindy moved back to the little house she bought during her first days in Seattle. Even though they shared 50-50 custody, little six-year-old Michael was a constant thought when he was not in her presence. This arrangement did provide Cindy the time to start the nonprofit Schools for Salone and recruit an active board of directors headed by Bob Heavner. During its first two years, the infant organization built three schools in Sierra Leone villages.

CINDY'S FAVORITE QUOTES

"Never doubt that a small group of thoughtful, committed citizens can change the world; indeed, it's the only thing that ever has."

~ Margaret Mead,
American Cultural Anthropologist

Today, through generous supporters, engaged board members, and a single commitment to provide first access, basic education to mostly rural villages in Sierra Leone,

Schools for Salone has built 25 schools and three libraries. Despite their simple design -- 50 feet deep and 120 feet long, with three classrooms and a small office that doubles as a library – each school can provide a first through-fourth-grade education for 200 children. Most village families have multiple children, but for the most part only one from each family can attend as the others must continue to farm and try to generate income for the family. Few of the mud-stick-and-thatched-roof houses in the villages are without multiple generations living inside. In addition to the hundreds of children and village leaders, it is the friends and confidants guiding her in the U.S. and other developed countries who are the reason Cindy has returned to Sierra Leone every year since 2004. Of notable influence, are David Harrison and his wife. David is a retired professor from the University of Washington's Evans School of Public Policy and Governance. Without David's unending love, guidance, and commitment to see Cindy develop her organization to its fullest potential, Schools for Salone might never have become the organization it is today. Cindy's feelings are the same for Joseph Lemin. His organization Programme for Children has been the key to getting her work accomplished throughout Sierra Leone, a country whose systems were not built for progress. Cindy credits these deep friendships and her education as the reason she is able to lead Schools for Salone to where it is today.

Cindy's father encouraged her to study physical therapy after she earned her bachelor's degree at Hood College in

Maryland. Observing the careers of her father, a hospital chaplain, and her mother, a registered nurse, Cindy was sure neither one of those professions would be her choice. Her mother's advice was to choose an occupation that would enable Cindy to make a living should something happen to a future husband. Cindy took her counsel and earned her Master's Degree in physical therapy from Boston University. But Cindy was not done exploring the desire to learn and discover. Following a passion for animals, specifically horses, she applied and was accepted to veterinary school in Blacksburg, Virginia. With little support from family because of the enormous debt she would incur and her own realization that being a vet could not provide the same flexibility as being a physical therapist, she withdrew after just one quarter. After a move to Seattle, Cindy enrolled in the University of Washington Masters' in Health Administration program, a degree that's provided some benefits when analyzing the needs of villagers in Sierra Leone.

Throughout her journey on both sides of the Atlantic, Cindy has been given plenty of ideas, advice, and feedback from people near and far. Through the process of trying to incorporate the concepts of others, she's learned several important lessons. The first is to follow *your own* heart, not someone else's. Another is *who you are is just fine*. These two wayfinders have kept Cindy and Schools for Salone pointed in the singular direction to educate the children of Sierra Leone. One of the places Cindy's heart led her was to her board chair Bob Heavner, Ph.D. Both had experienced failures in first marriages, but together they shared progress and accomplishment in building Schools for Salone. With formidable experiences in Sierra Leone as Peace Corps volunteers and common commitments to the villages they served in, a special union grew between them. The two eventually married.

CINDY'S FAVORITE QUOTES

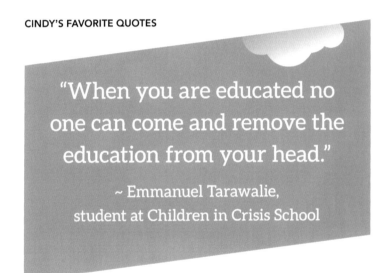

"When you are educated no one can come and remove the education from your head."

~ Emmanuel Tarawalie,
student at Children in Crisis School

Bob and Cindy provided a more serene environment for Michael than Cindy and Ken, her previous husband, could. The benefit of that calm and the relationship with his father, grandmother and a dozen close friends, has created an excellent student and world citizen of Michael. He's made six trips to Sierra Leone with Cindy and accepts that as a part of his unique life journey. Cindy has found her own calm and acceptance through an eclectic faith collective. With both mother and father Mennonite, husband one and two Jewish, and lots of friends practicing various other faiths, Cindy believes God lives in all of us. She particularly loves how Muslims and Christians in Sierra Leone not only practice faith side by side but also tolerate the open celebration of each other's sacred religious traditions.

Cindy cannot imagine the progress of Schools for Salone without her association to several community organizations both in the U.S. and Africa. These groups are the gateway to some of her most-cherished friends. Cindy also sees how these alliances will improve Michael's life as he charts his future course. Cindy credits the inspiration she gets from watching others doing life-changing work in the world as the momentum that has sustained her energy for Schools for Salone. Much of that enthusiasm to keep going is fueled by the impact Cindy has seen in this tiny West African nation that loves to learn.

Others have taken notice, too. In 2012, Cindy Nofziger received Washington state's Jefferson Award, a "Nobel Prize" of public service, for her work in Sierra Leone.

When Cindy sees what Sierra Leone has endured just in her lifetime, to include a decade-plus of devastating civil war, the Ebola epidemic, and a government that makes no priority to educate its children, her passion to provide Joseph and his team the resources they need only gets stronger. Without a doubt though, the strongest call back to Sierra Leone for Cindy are those smart, bright-eyed children on the playground in Maforeka screaming *Seen dee! Seen dee!*

CINDY NOFZIGER

Compassionate
Fun · Engaging
Committed · Loving
Active · Musical

PAUL "MOOSELIPS" DUDLEY

> I've never met anyone so committed to getting extraordinary children to smile either with a camera, a song, or a giant hug. Moose is the only man I know that spends most of his time standing with families trying to navigate the path of pediatric cancer treatment. ~ L. S.

Every June and July, the appropriately named marine vessel, *M/V Goodtimes II*, picks up a load of excited kids at the Vashon Island ferry dock, just an hour west of Seattle. The 120 passengers, ages 7-17 years old, are all very good at celebrating life. Many of them, and their families, have a different value of time. The Goodtimes Project is a non-profit organization dedicated to supporting children in Western Washington and Alaska that are dealing with pediatric cancer. These kids and their loved ones know every day is a gift. The week at Camp Goodtimes allows them to make memories with others who value each day in a similar way.

Docking the 87-foot *M/V Goodtimes II* into the landing is the same captain who's been at the helm for 25 years.

Paul Dudley, or as he is known to campers, "Mooselips," gets great joy watching his youthful, brightly-dressed, neon-adorned passengers jump aboard. This isn't the only time his special guests will see him during their week at Camp Goodtimes. "Mooselips," also called "Moose" by many, will be their director of fun morning, noon, and night. Like dozens of volunteers and his dedicated staff, the week at camp each summer helps Moose acknowledge that time is not infinite. Every volunteer and staff member shares Moose's mission of serving these fantastic kids who are battling different forms of pediatric cancer. These kids' week at Camp Goodtimes will be the most fun they've ever had. From the moment they awake until they collapse after dark, they'll enjoy nonstop games and celebrations. Moose accepts his daily role full-force. There's usually a guitar, Twinkies, bubbles, whipped cream, hair color, bean bags, and glow-in-the-dark paint included. Some kids come to camp in celebration of a family member lost to cancer. Camp Goodtimes hosts siblings or those who have lost one in the recent past.

Much of the programming at the one-week camp is rooted in fun. Several other benefits come from kids spending time around others, who, like themselves, are impacted by cancer: connection, personal growth, and the chance to find other kids on a similar path. For the families who have been managing a treatment schedule and the rest of life, Camp Goodtimes is a chance to breathe, knowing the on-site medical staff is able to care for each child's plethora of needs.

Moose is sure the medicine of smiles, laughs, and pranks is best taken in large doses. The other therapy he knows well is song. Every camper leaves with an entire songbook of new tunes in their head, many taken in around each evening's campfire with plenty of s'mores. The non-stop activities at Camp Goodtimes use every ounce of Moose's midlife energy. Lucky for him, his family and friends are built on strength and longevity, including Captain Lynn Campbell, who hired Moose into his Harbor Tour Company in 1978 when Moose was just 19. Harbor Tour Company would later be renamed Argosy Cruises, a popular tour boat company still thriving in Seattle.

Captain Lynn was everything Moose wanted to be. His personality was larger than life, he had a booming voice, and a giant heart. As he taught Moose the techniques of moving a 100-ton ship around the Puget Sound in Washington, Captain Campbell wasn't afraid to quickly correct the apprentice's failures but was also very good at celebrating each success. Beyond being a fantastic teacher of maritime best practices, Captain Lynn imparted some of the best leadership lessons Moose has ever learned. Much of the confidence Moose is using to lead in life and business today is courtesy of the man who gave Moose his first shot at the nautical wheel. Few days pass that Moose isn't demonstrating his appreciation for all that Captain Lynn gifted him before his passing at age 101 in late 2013. Those treasures include: a belief in others, confidence in your own ability, celebrating even the smallest achievements, taking the time to look someone directly in the eye, and really showing that you care about them and what they have to say. These are the attributes a seaworthy captain passed to his first mate over four decades ago.

Another centenarian that influenced Moose to be the best version of himself was his grandmother, Loulie. Even though they saw each other just a handful of times a year, Loulie set him up for life by sharing her wisdom and outlook on humanity. She, too, instilled a sense of confidence in Moose by always reminding him she believed in who he was and most importantly, who he was becoming. Living in the nation's capital, Loulie was surprised that Moose didn't jump at the chance to visit the significant museums within a short distance of her home when he came to see her. He always reminded Grandma Loulie that the one-on-one times sitting at her dining room table imparted many more lessons than the halls of a museum, regardless of the artist. One of Loulie's life lessons Moose uses often is to never leave anything unsaid. This has helped him as husband, father, and as a leader of children whose paths aren't always certain. Moose gives his own mother, Abigail, much of the credit for his drive to make a difference in the world. His compassionate call to help those in need, an optimistic view of the future, and an ability to add hope to a situation that would seem hopeless to the majority is because of his mom. Between Grandma Loulie, his mom, Captain Campbell, and dozens of other wise souls, Moose is the first to admit his life has been inspired by others. In his daily movements as a professional photographer, philanthropy/fundraising evangelist, and lifetime volunteer walking beside families trying to navigate the spectrum of emotions that come with their children's cancer journey, Moose regularly exercises the gifts passed to him by this impactful collection of family and friends.

MOOSE'S FAVORITE QUOTES

> "Are we not beings, joined together through bonds of emotion, to create and share the joy of being alive?"
>
> ~ Paul Dudley, journal entry 1979

The lessons of his formal education have also added much to who Moose is today. He spent plenty of time learning to love philosophy and anthropology. Combined with his earlier family education, Moose finds it not so ironic that the root of the word *philanthropy* is the same as *philosophy* and that *anthropology*, traced to its original roots, translates to "Love of Mankind." A second and just-as-fitting definition of his keen ability to get donors to invest in charitable causes is: To Promote the Welfare of Others. Much of that mission is accomplished as Moose regularly stands before audiences as a fundraising host and auctioneer asking them to support important causes, most of them to benefit children's cancer charities, Camp Goodtimes among them.

MOOSE'S FAVORITE QUOTES

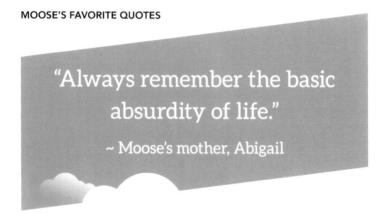

"Always remember the basic absurdity of life."

~ Moose's mother, Abigail

A self-generated thought still serving him well long after its youthful origin is, "When in doubt—go for it." Moose endeavors not to take life too seriously, but also to push through even when the proposal has a minority chance of coming to fruition. It is an outlook built on possibility and hope, a feature of life Moose has seen plenty of families hang their hats on while walking the uneven path of cancer treatments and results. Through many lessons, both early in life and now at mid-life, he's determined some of his life truths. The first is take the time to listen carefully to your heart. The second is to look at the world with caring eyes. The third is to try to listen to what's in others' hearts to find out how to help them best. The fourth is being able to be critical of yourself with the target of learning and growing. Finally, Moose believes it's most important to be able to ask yourself the most honest and brutal questions. This process is only valid if there is a willingness to give yourself an answer with as much honesty as was in the question.

These are the values Moose brings to his 34-year marriage with Heidi, and to parenting of his two children — son, Miles, and daughter, Alex. Moose knows Heidi will always be there for him, no matter what the endeavor. Also, as has happened in the past, when the results aren't as predicted, she helps Moose regroup and is the first to encourage a new, more productive path. Both Heidi and Moose have plenty of vivid examples close to them that elevate their appreciation for every day. Each of them acknowledges it as a gift. They also celebrate the combined values that show up in their kids' lives. In addition to living the joy of seeing their 23-year-old son graduating college and their 17-year-old daughter starting her university days, Moose has gratitude for his children's sense of confidence and drive, two qualities he doesn't remember possessing at their age.

Faith is also an aspect of Moose's life that has been front and center. He believes faith has a handful of touchpoints in his world. The first is trust, in himself and others. Following that is belief, confidence, and conviction. Each of those qualities inspires Moose to live each day with hope for himself, his family, and the dozens of special kids he is privileged to help. Another pair of attributes associated to his faith are action and a dose of urgency, especially for those whose future is uncertain.

MOOSE'S FAVORITE QUOTES

"Life hangs by a thread...who is to say that we will be alive tomorrow ...so let us be happy today."

~ Unknown, in a 1950's Hercules movie

When it comes to business, living each day as it happens would be a good way to describe Moose's written goals and business plan. This form of unbridled strategy has served Moose well for nearly all his life. As a sought-after wedding, event and portrait photographer, Moose has been able to share the room and studio with several of America's most admired people, including Oprah, President Obama and First Lady Michelle, Bill Gates, and Elton John.

Over the past 30 years, Moose has turned his volunteer time behind the camera into a gift for families that have lost a child to cancer. His careful, thoughtful, and personal skill set captures a set of photographs families can treasure forever. Moose also does some of his best camera work documenting moments of happiness and joy when one of the kids finishes a long course of treatments.

It's hard for Moose to look too far forward and work toward something that's not in full view today. To Moose, the process of achieving something significant is more important than the future prize. Moose stays present because he knows that's where need is the greatest. Supporting families that need him in one way or another is his way of looking down the road. Knowing he's serving something much bigger than himself keeps Moose content. His mom spent plenty of time getting Moose ready for the day he would meet that first kid with cancer. Moose feels like he was there at the right time and had the ability to help. Grandma Loulie tried to prepare Moose with the tools to spot where he could leave his mark. Neither she nor Moose knew what that would look like, but now, thousands of Camp Goodtimes kids and dozens of hours behind the wheel on Puget Sound later, the picture is clear. There is no doubt Captain Lynn is looking down from Heaven, watching his first mate make him proud.

PAUL "MOOSELIPS" DUDLEY

Trustworthy
Results Oriented
Powerful · Positive
Compassionate
Wise

TONI SCOTT MIHAL

It's incredible for me to watch Toni lift up people from one side of the world to the other. She has improved lives through her extraordinary and faithful, Jesus-centered mission work. ~ L. S.

W hen Toni Scott Mihal says she's on a mission, that's an understatement. She's actually on six missions, all at the same time. Supplying hungry people with a week's worth of nutritious food is the objective of the nearest mission. Trying to improve communities decimated by Aids in Swaziland, South Africa is her long distance run. Toni is a one-women force, Missions Director at Church on the Ridge, in an active community an hour east of Seattle. Her large faith community sees it as their calling to impact sex trafficking of young women in Latvia, impoverished children living in desperate conditions in Cambodia, rebuilding small communities to sustain themselves in Honduras, and shepherds of a fellow faith community in Swaziland. Toni knows these places well. She's the missionary who maintains the relationships with both the faithful in the field and those who assemble at home to support them.

Each facet of her work requires a unique perspective due to the population her mission supports.

In Riga, Latvia's capital city, where prostitution is legal and contributes to the economy with an estimated 7,500 prostitutes, Toni's mission partner, Freedom61, attempts to show the girls a higher value and better human experience by operating a café in the very district where most of the girls sell themselves. Conversations over coffee offer the girls a path out of prostitution and into a rehabilitation and transition center two hours outside Riga. Toni's annual trip to Latvia gives her renewed confidence that although Riga is still a historic capital city hosting large amounts of sex tourism, at least the girls have an option for another way of life. In Southeast Asia, Toni's mission to rescue children living in a giant Cambodian landfill and get them into decent housing is her priority. Her organization also hosts a women's ministry and a feeding center in one of the most impoverished parts of Cambodia. Toni knows it's faith that draws her to these hopeless spots. She also knows it's faith that will power the change and movement to a more actualized life for her people there.

This year marks an important milestone for Toni's mission work in Asia. For the first time, with the help of another faith-centered mission group, Toni's organization will host a country-wide youth camp in Cambodia to share the word of God. Few places Toni visits are as deprived of resources as Swaziland. With nearly 50% of the population infected with AIDS, this tiny nation between South Africa and Mozambique exists in a constant state of despair. Toni is able to provide hope and needed strength by supporting those who teach, farm, and minister. Her supporters recently funded a tractor used to generate farm income. The proceeds are used to support both the families and the pastor in a local, community church. With such loss and suffering, faith and gratitude are held in high standing throughout Swaziland. Toni does her best to provide them plenty of reasons to be hopeful which is why she and her team travel there. Being able to make a meaningful impact in Swaziland doesn't require as much funding but does require much more prayer with so many forces pushing them backwards. Between AIDS, famine, corruption, weather patterns that impact farming, and shortages of nearly everything, miracles are born from the faithful supported by Toni's mission.

Another nation full of challenges that Toni and her team lift up is Honduras. Ministering in rural, Central American villages to reconstruct the physical and spiritual brokenness after years of civil war and decay keeps Toni and her missions team plenty occupied during their annual visits. Each of these far-away missions has needs well beyond what Toni's team and partners can satisfy. Without significant faith and generous giving among the congregation on Sunday, these missions simply could not continue.

Not all the impact of Toni's mission work requires a long flight. An hour south of Church on the Ridge is a place of second chances, renewal and grace. Toni's support of

Teen Challenge aims to help young women break the cycle of addiction through discipleship, personal responsibility and mentorship. The yearlong program provides each resident the tools to find a new, more productive path including tapping into the strength from a personal relationship with Jesus. A center piece of Toni's work with Teen Challenge is organizing an annual Christmas event to make sure the teens feel loved during a time of year that can create isolation for many, especially those trying to maintain addiction recovery. Between gifts, a full holiday meal, and the announcement of Christ's birth in a manger, each girl comes to feel the reason for the season. Toni's time is also spent feeding hungry people in the local community. Each week, through the valiant efforts of one part-time employee and hundreds of committed volunteers, the Mt Si Food Bank serves 1,100 people who wouldn't ordinarily have access to a quality, consistent food supply. This includes 200 children in local schools that benefit from a well-organized backpack program meant to be their food safety net. The food supply is an outpouring from the local merchants and suppliers that realize there are mouths to feed in the very neighborhood in which they live. Toni and her army of Food Bank volunteers spend 650 hours every month making sure everyone has enough to eat.

Toni's family support for all her moving about starts at home. Husband, Jeff, who maintains another leadership post at Church on the Ridge, is Toni's biggest advocate and cheerleader. Missions work can be emotionally, physically, and spiritually tough. Jeff lifts Toni in spirit and grace by reminding her of the impact she's made on others in the farthest reaches of the world. Jeff's love of God is also a source of strength Toni regularly leans on when times get too challenging. Toni finds it particularly inspiring to observe Jeff's servant leadership, always putting other's needs first.

TONI'S FAVORITE QUOTES

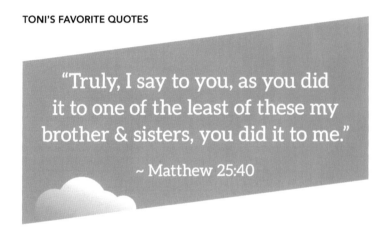

"Truly, I say to you, as you did it to one of the least of these my brother & sisters, you did it to me."

~ Matthew 25:40

Both Jeff and Toni are trying to be an example for their two young daughters. It's Toni's and Jeff's goal to live the example they wish their kids to be. Toni also wants her children to see that just because mom and dad work, that doesn't mean one or both parents are always absent. The girls get plenty of opportunity to be part of nearly all the activities the large Church on the Ridge congregation provides for the community. Toni wants her girls to grow up and be women of faith and action. Her commitment and passion for Jesus wasn't always present. Her perception of the people living through their faith was skewed with images of parishioners acting odd, pushing Bibles in the faces of those not interested. That was until she met Jeff. He was already living through his faith in God but not at all in the way Toni imagined it would look. Toni's preconceived notions were dismissed. The more time she spent with Jeff, the easier it became for her to see that faith is a dynamic belief system that requires constant, selfless service to others, especially the ones that don't look like you. Toni's calling to missions came as a bit of a surprise to her. While scanning the pages of upcoming events in her church program, an announcement about a team forming to travel and minister in Cambodia stopped her page turning. As she imagined why anyone in the world would leave the comfortable confines of America to try and survive in a developing country, Toni says the voice of God spoke to her and said Go! This wasn't a soft suggestion, but more a directive to go and become a pilgrim of His work. Toni tried to dismiss the idea as she struggled with a dozen reasons why she shouldn't go, including the needs of her family at home. Jeff, of course, thought it was a fantastic idea and was the first to encourage her to join the team. That first mission trip changed the course of Toni's life. Subsequent mission trips to Cambodia, Latvia, Swaziland, and Honduras re-formed the shape of Toni's heart and put Jesus in the center of her soul. Recognizing the power of that first calling, Toni began listening for further guidance from up above. She could see, hear, and feel that serving in the missions field was feeding her life even more than it was feeding the people she went to serve.

Inspired by others living in the mission field full time, Toni was pondering if that was the life plan she and her family should be following. Not long after, the Director of Missions role came open. Toni took it and is now able to live in the land of abundance and share it among programs she leads. Having grown up in a very small town, Toni sees missions as a way to broaden her perspective and become part of larger communities like the dozens of families that support Church on the Ridge.

TONI'S FAVORITE QUOTES

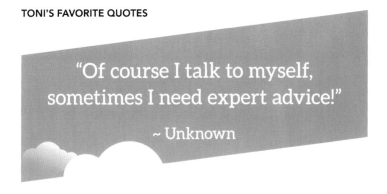

"Of course I talk to myself, sometimes I need expert advice!"

~ Unknown

Toni had a rural upbringing with just 36 students in her high school graduating class. She saw college as a way out of small town America. Her appreciation for education is immense, especially coupled with life experiences like studying aboard and avoiding the need to rush though her classes in four years. The most important benefit of taking her time getting to graduation day was meeting Jeff, which wouldn't have happened if Toni had taken the path most in her class traveled. That reduced pace has served Toni well in life and she believes more could benefit from a reduced speed when it comes to how she sees accomplished people doing important work in the world. Her view is all about the example others show using whatever time is needed to put other's needs ahead of her own. Toni also believes that being outstanding in one's chosen pursuits requires faith, patience, and the knowledge that blessings come to those who ask for them. Of course, Toni and Jeff's daughters are that blessing for them. Raising young girls in today's digital society advances their expectation of life and isn't forgiving around identity and image. Even with those facets everyday pushing their girls faster than Toni remembers from her small-town childhood, she and Jeff are confident their daughters will grow up to be strong women of faith.

Like most marriages, the nearly-two-decade union between Toni and Jeff has seen challenges. As a couple, they've leaned on their collective faith to weather more than one storm and the kids haven't been blind to the struggle. Fortunately, Toni and Jeff have made it clear to both girls that these days of trouble are another opportunity to strengthen as a family and give thanks to God for being able to lean on Him for grace. Toni is the first to admit their challenges to continue as a happily married couple have only made her appreciate and love her husband even more, especially during the moments when she had a tough time accepting his unconditional love of her. Much of what Toni has learned on this journey toward unison as a couple is beneficial both at home and in the missions office. Writing things down is one valuable lesson.

TONI'S FAVORITE QUOTES

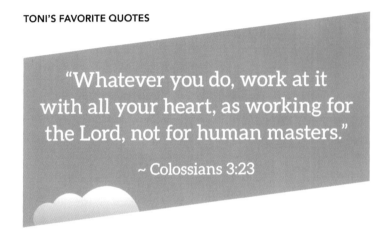

"Whatever you do, work at it with all your heart, as working for the Lord, not for human masters."

~ Colossians 3:23

Through a professional development initiative, the church began a process of writing and scoring WIGS or Wildly Important Goals. Starting a daily tally in her office every day, Toni's priorities became closely focused on making decisions around her specific set of goals. Through this systematic, written, achievement process, Toni is able to celebrate the victories and learn from the losses. One of Toni's WIGS for her faith community is to be on a mission, all the time. Loving neighbors, feeding the hungry, and visiting the sick, are the goals she's asking her congregation to put into action. Toni believes this is a mission worth achieving partly because no one needs to board an airplane and also, this WIG is right in the backyard of everyone that attends on Sunday.

Even without having to travel out of the area to be on this mission, her members do have to leave their spiritual comfort zone. Toni has seen it is almost easier to love another person who doesn't speak your same language and who you may never see again than it is to love the person on the other size of the fence in your own cul-de-sac. Toni believes this mission is the one that will bring her community closer and bring a few people out of their shells. A self-confessed introvert, Toni had to make a significant shift in her comfort facing people when she said yes to her current post. In the end, her role is to engage with people she's never met and let them know, no matter how difficult their current circumstance, she is there to help or will find someone that can.

Seeing communities near and far transformed by her teams is the ultimate motivation for Toni and everyone involved. Locally, a team of women crochet plastic bags into sleeping matts for homeless youth. Others diligently pick up donated food for those that depend on Toni's food bank to keep their families fed. In Swaziland, a tractor funded by Toni's faithful keeps a pastor in a church, and kids in Cambodia will go to camp for the first time. Missions work isn't for everyone and most of the time there's not significant praise or recognition of the work. When Toni does receive kudos about how her ministry has turned a life in the right direction she stores it for a time when she's got nothing left in the tank. In the end though, Toni knows the only approval she really needs is from the Lord above.

TONI SCOTT MIHAL

STEVE

**Curiosity • Tenacity
Strategist • Humor • Coffee
Easily Distracted**

MELODY

**Kind • Big Heart
Empathetic • Stubborn
Hard Working**

STEVE / MELODY EDMISTON

This is, by far, the strongest couple I've ever met. Extraordinary in so many, ways including three near-death experiences with cancer; they have used each to fortify the union between them. ~ L. S.

Woodmont is a two-street berg nestled on the shores of the Puget Sound. Melody and Steve's living room looks out over hourly changes in the busy South Sound's shipping lanes. Were you to look the opposite direction, back through the window at Steve and Melody, your view would take in even more change. You'd see the kind of life-altering shifts that require serious human strength, unbridled confidence in others, and a kind of commitment reserved for only those willing to go the distance.

For nearly a dozen years, Steve and Melody, with daughters Paige and Madison, have been in a family fight. This isn't the typical battle that sends family members to different corners of a city never to speak again. It is the kind of conflict that's done everything to make them stronger and battle hardened: cancer. Lots of it. Over-and-over again.

Hearing the words "Stage 4 Hodgkin's Lymphoma" from Steve's oncologist sent Melody to the only place she could find peace on earth: lying next to her mom and shedding every tear possible for most of an entire day. Melody then gathered herself together, drove to pick up her two young girls at school and never looked back.

MELODY'S FAVORITE QUOTES

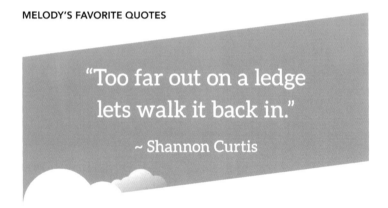

"Too far out on a ledge lets walk it back in."

~ Shannon Curtis

Wanting to live in the present without looking too far forward has become Melody's strategy in playing the hand of cards she and Steve have been dealt. Their parents also play central roles in how this batch of unfortunate circumstances plays out. Steve and Melody both draw strength and love from their appreciation of their stable childhoods. Both of their moms could have easily taken home lifetime achievement awards for holding their homes together through their own set of family issues. Finding inspiration and support from watching their parents fight through medical and social challenges has equipped Steve and Melody to face an endless path of their own medical challenges.

Navigating the uneven sidewalk of cancer treatment takes hope, love of all things one values, and the ability to borrow strength from others when your own tank is way past empty. Steve's cancer ravaged him, then seemed to be defeated, then returned to batter his body and soul again. Leading Steve's fight through his set of near-death experiences from the very beginning has been an extraordinary man who is so much more than an oncologist. Dr. Henry "Hank" Kaplan took countless calls on weekends, advocated Steve's case with other medical professionals, pushed the slow-moving insurance system, interrupted his family vacations, and went all in for the future of Team Edmiston. Many days were spent in a clinic room waiting for Dr. Kaplan to appear. None of them are as memorable as the fateful day following Steve's first set of treatments for Stage 4 Hodgkin's Lymphoma.

Oncologists are asked to weigh in on many questions while in a family huddle. Nearly all of them possess the same intention, with hope being the primary ingredient. Dr. Kaplan had been the quarterback in this huddle multiple times a day. He'd been asked to respond to questions that most of the time have no clear or time-defined answers. He balances the reality that is cancer with the only medicine his patients can generate for themselves: hope. Steve and Melody know how to create hope better than most. For a decade, each day has been a sincere lesson in shaping medical reports into hope. As Dr. Kaplan appeared in the room for this update, hope and fear each had a spot in Steve and Melody's minds. Dr. Kaplan gave them the news. Hope grew, and fear diminished. Steve wanted to stand on the side of the field that had no end in sight. Dr. Kaplan's update gave him that view. From that moment forward, a brotherhood of doctor and patient was established.

Steve's battles with cancer have lasted a decade, and more. He is possessed with an ability to find hope and hold to it and live off it, but he has also been blessed with a solid foundation of extraordinary allies in Melody, Paige, Madison, and Dr. Kaplan.

With the confidence that there will be many days ahead, the family could now spend more days supporting each other's gifts. Super Mom Melody keeps everything on track. Dad, an accomplished attorney, screenwriter, and film and TV producer spends most of his waking hours in creative mode. Twenty-something daughters Paige and Madison have taken this special family DNA mix and carved out their own unique trail. Seeking to elevate and reward the life experience of others, Paige, along with plenty of family guidance, founded *The Sidekick Collective*. Inspired by an essay that she wrote in high school positing that superheroes don't just live in comic books, Paige believes true superheroes exist in the real world too. She and friends reward high school students with seed funding for solid ideas that make a difference in the communities where they live. This form of Hero Capitalism doesn't follow a common path of reward for work well done. Through a peer nomination process, the Cosmic Hero award is a surprise to the recipient. With Melody serving as Board President, and Steve as Director of Hero Relations, Legal Affairs, *The Sidekick Collective* is very much a family mission at the Edmiston house. Madison has an extraordinary eye behind the camera and a well-formed, high quality, journalistic skillset too. Each year the family and *The Sidekick Collective* Board of Directors review dozens of nominations looking for those that embody the qualities of a community change agent. This creative, game changing, collective effect is nothing new at the Edmiston address.

MELODY'S FAVORITE QUOTES

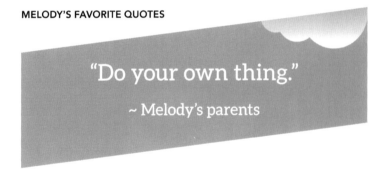

"Do your own thing."

~ Melody's parents

Community activism has brought Steve, Melody and family to the kitchen table many times over. Seeking answers of elected officials, neighborhood leaders, and citizens alike, the Edmiston family has never been afraid to use their collective, well-informed voices to get answers for the rest of us. Steve recognizes that each of his ideas, no matter the scale, needs the blessing of the woman who has been by his side for nearly 40 years. One of the most important assessments Melody brings is the possibility of success or failure. With this all in, pass-or-fail grading scheme, Steve has been able to invest the time needed to bring several motion picture projects to market. For them both, the confidence to create is in part due to the value and practice of continued learning.

STEVE'S FAVORITE QUOTES

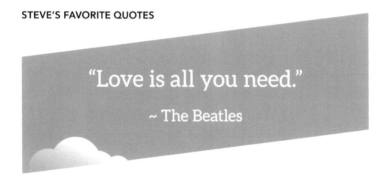

"Love is all you need."

~ The Beatles

Steve has a keen drive to add new mental content at a pace quicker than most, born from the need to be always evolving into the best of whatever is put before him at any given moment. Steve's intersection of law, film, entrepreneurship, activism, fatherhood, and being a husband fuels his insatiable love of learning from others. Like other endeavors, he sees learning as a journey with limitless potential. Steve stands before aspiring filmmakers and screenwriters to share his passion for taking an idea all the way to the big screen. His evangelism for intellectual curiosity, tenacity, sweat, and hard work inspire nearly anyone who will listen to him.

As much as they both love learning, there is a teacher living inside each of them, as well. Melody spends her professional day trying to get forgotten youth to find a trail that will lead to a better destination than the current one they're on. She tries to get kids and what's left of their families to focus on their strengths and not what's been holding them back. Working with marginalized youth who hold little value for education enables Melody to regularly visit the healthy respect she has for learning. Being curious is what fuels her need to learn and be informed. She is the first to share her gratitude for each day her feet hit the floor, to accept what has been, what lies ahead, and what is currently happening.

STEVE'S FAVORITE QUOTES

> "Let us therefor study the incidents in this as philosophy to learn wisdom, and none of them as wrongs to be revenged."
>
> ~ Abraham Lincoln

One of the most important teaching moments in both Steve's and Melody's need to share, began in the four walls of their own home. An early family value that still pays interest every day for the whole clan is: *Be nice to everyone.* As proud parents, they have countless stories of seeing both daughters practicing this family mantra. Steve and Melody have allowed others to influence their family's outcome. Two of the most useful counsel included are: *Accept your path head-on* and *don't spend precious time wishing for anything else.* Another set of words Melody's father never let her forget is: *Nobody has the answers for you. Go find them yourself. You have everything you need.* Even though that set of words caused her frustration in her youth, today Melody uses it as her rallying cry to get things accomplished. Steve has been the beneficiary of mind-shifting advice from all angles. As a voracious reader, he's been able to process many an author's good and intentional words of advice. His favorite is: *If you work hard in a passionate pursuit of a significant goal, amazing results will come.*

Both Steve and Melody acknowledge faith as an important source of strength and love. Even though Melody has experienced shifts in faith, her unending belief that something bigger is at work has never wavered. She looks forward to the day when the picture all comes together. Steve maintains that God is the only true way to explain love. No surprise, faith for him can be best defined in a line from *Les Misérables: To love another person is to see the face of God.* This acknowledgment of a greater existence and the gratitude that comes with it has been an important factor when looking back at accomplishments and goals attained.

Rooted in her earliest memories of church, Melody was given the gift of service to others. Her grandparents gathered church members to fill the community gap. Melody has come to count on a special set of confidants she gathered in college. Today, they truly know, challenge, and support each other. The shape of Melody's life today is due to this sisterhood she's had for more than half of her life. When Steve reflects on the influence of community organizations on the shape of his world, he simply cannot imagine where he would be without them. Be it film forums or festivals, entrepreneurs or innovators, his world has truly lived off the creative tension needed to accomplish artistic endeavors.

As Melody and Steve look toward the future, it's not difficult to identify what will keep them inspired and motivated. For Melody, it's the consistent mission to make today better than yesterday for those she serves, including Steve, Paige, Madison and a new Springer Spaniel named Emmy Lou. Serving those who need it most in and outside her house helps ensure that the world will continue to spin in her favor. Keeping a family intact when fate has tested its strength and longevity helps Melody strive to be the best version of herself, every day. Little did Steve realize the personal application of the prophetic words of Simon and Garfunkel on the day he said *I do*. Pastor Ben Lindstrom was right. Steve married up.

STEVE'S FAVORITE QUOTES

"Your time has come to shine
All your dreams are on their way
See how they shine
Oh, if you need a friend
I'm sailing right behind
Like a bridge over troubled water
I will ease your mind"

~ Simon and Garfunkel

Because he's stared down the end of his own path three times and is still walking, Steve has no problem staying fired up about the long term with a close eye on today. Being able to create, and support those that do and create, keeps him fully engaged in the projects at hand. Family, friends, and a new beautiful four-legged addition to the nest give Steve all the gifts for which he could possibly ask.

STEVE / MELODY EDMISTON

**Driven • Caring
Creative • Excitable
Decisive • Integrity
Inspirational
Accountable**

CHEF JOHN HOWIE

I've been inspired watching the generosity that Chef John Howie extends to guests, employees, and community members. His work in the kitchen and in the world is extraordinary! ~ L. S.

Any savvy diner in the Seattle area has heard of Chef John Howie, and likely eaten at one of his Seattle-area tables. Nationally recognized by countless publications, radio and television shows, Howie has received numerous prestigious awards for his cooking and menus.

Normally, the most important ingredients in a renowned restaurant like Howie's are kept hidden in the kitchen. However, John Howie keeps his number-one-preferred recipe, that of philanthropy, wide open in his heart. In 2017 alone, his philanthropic community alliances fed more than one million hungry people. Not one of those people paid a dime for their meals. Howie says, "My strongest direction stems from the graceful hand of God, which I believe is pointing me toward continuing to be a major contributor to my employees and the community."

Howie also credits his success to three key practices:

identifying business plans, aligning these with specific, personal goals, and having the willingness to be flexible when meeting those targets. The best guidance he's received from a mentor is to "never rest on your laurels."

Much of Chef John Howie's journey can be traced back to a fateful day: October 10, 1963. Returning home from a family day on the farm with too many pumpkins stuffed into his Volkswagen Beetle, John's father couldn't fit his son in the car. Tragically, just ten minutes later, a Chevy station wagon rammed into the Volkswagen and John's father died instantly. John was just a dozen days from his fourth birthday.

John's father had been a Captain with United Airlines. During his commercial flying days, he'd met a flight attendant who would later become his wife, and John's mother. In addition to flying domestic routes for United, the elder Howie was also a real estate agent and farmer, setting an early example for John as an entrepreneur.

Although John's father's life was cut short, he left a legacy behind that his son lives to honor through his daily actions as an entrepreneur, devoted husband, and father of two sons. Through his father's example, instilled in him by way of stories about his father's life, Chef Howie learned the value of time and purpose. John has also taken inspiration from his mother's strength. Losing the love of her life and raising three small children as a single mom was not an easy task.

Following a traditional educational route wasn't a

viable option for John as he needed to contribute his time and resources to his mother at home. But after receiving a GED from Bellevue Community College and taking a select number of business courses, John found his best learning experience, and where his passion excelled, was in the restaurant kitchen.

CHEF HOWIE'S FAVORITE QUOTES

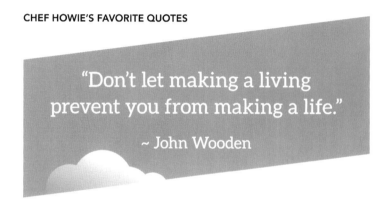

"Don't let making a living prevent you from making a life."

~ John Wooden

Chef Howie's professional life was shaped through early lessons in tenacity and drive. He learned his first set of business principles while selling Cutco knives door to door with kindred-spirit school buddy Steve Wasser. Both John and Steve grew up in homes with a single parent and shared a deep desire to achieve success. John was deeply inspired as he watched Steve take advantage of his spot in the land of opportunity. From knives, to roofing, to advertising, and onward to a well-known consulting practice traveling the country helping others realize their goals, Steve provided John with plenty of examples of how to hit his own targets.

When Bellevue's Seastar Restaurant and Raw Bar, the first of its kind in the area, was only a dream in Chef Howie's heart, Steve provided one of the initial investments to make it a reality.

Two restaurant industry mentors continue to guide John's insatiable desire to keep his world calm, profitable, and balanced. Working alongside Chef Garret Cho has enabled John to see that loyalty, attention to quality, and admirable culinary skills are key ingredients to running a successful kitchen. Another inspiration to John was having the honor of working with the highly influential restaurateur, RUI (Restaurant Unlimited Incorporated) founder, Rich Komen. Widely regarded by John and many others as one of the best in the business, the former University of Washington Husky Stadium peanut man provided a set of guiding principles that ran through every level of his company:

- **The first:** listen to your guests. The customer is the one that will tell you what you're doing right and what you're doing wrong.

- **The second:** you simply cannot do everything yourself. Hire the very best you can find, give them direction and let them do their work.

Chef Komen's principles continue to influence Chef Howie and his dedicated staff. John credits them with his success in growing John Howie Restaurants since his first venture, Seastar, opened in 2002.

CHEF HOWIE'S FAVORITE QUOTES

> "Whether you think you can,
> or you think you can't, you're right!"
>
> ~ Henry Ford

Success in the restaurant business is notoriously elusive. When Chef Howie opened Seastar in 2002, its survival was not a forgone conclusion. To make it, John leaned on his early lessons. He then learned other lessons as the business grew, and several more through the years. Looking back at the rough patches of startup, at examples of underperforming staff members, he often assumes some of the responsibility. He realizes now that the poor performance he was getting from staff was, in part, due to his own failure to base his expectations on specific, agreed-upon time or training levels. He learned that getting the best version of each staff member required establishing a strategic system that included agreeing on a set of outcomes based on training to be completed within a specified amount of time.

Time has proven this management methodology to be quite effective. Chef Howie's restaurants retain employees for significantly longer than the industry average. Staff members, from the kitchen to the front of the house, willingly raise their hands to volunteer for a myriad of charitable fundraising events supported by John Howie Restaurants. Often, these events require employees to be even more hands-on than the role they are paid to fill. Chef Howie learned early on that reciprocal loyalty has significant benefits for the long-term connectivity to his team. He has asked more of his staff than most fine dining restaurateurs. But their extra effort doesn't go without notice or added praise, a practice John learned early on is key to consistent, repeatable, quality work.

Today, John and his trusted partners run a handful of first-class restaurants, a distillery, a brewery, and a collection of at-home cooking products. His values are closely aligned with his father's. John's desire to make his family proud, be generous to his community, and operate a respected company are his daily wayfinders. That same simple but sometimes tough-to-model standard applies at home too. As a husband, he is devoted. For twenty-seven years, he and his wife Debbie's care and compassion for others has also earned them a wide and deep pool of close friends. As a team, they've raised wonderful children, who in turn, are raising exemplary kids of their own.

John is proud of his sons. Eric's love of golf earned him a

spot on his high school golf team. He also brought the first of the next generation into the family circle. At nine-years-old, Eric's son Zac is already exhibiting the compassion of his grandmother, and, like his great-grandpa and grandpa, showing great respect to those around him.

John Harvey "Jo-Jo" Howie, Chef Howie's other son, showed passion for baseball early, developing into a standout pitcher. His accomplishments mirror his father's stalwart focus toward setting and achieving goals. Today, Jo-Jo's love for the game continues in his work as a college coach. Chef Howie's granddaughter, Violet, was born to Jo-Jo and his wife in 2015. Jo-Jo's birthday is a particularly special day in the Howie household. On May 31, 1991, Chef John shot his only hole in one. On that same day in 1993, Jo-Jo was born. Finally, on May 31, 2006, the first barrel of John Howie Bourdon Blend from Woodford Reserve was produced.

In addition to his marriage and family, John views his acceptance of Christ as a primary source of strength. He leans on God's word as his moral compass and as an essential ingredient to his accomplishments. Becoming more involved in his church and faith-centered men's groups have provided divine guidance when he needed it most. John's faith has shown him how having passion in everything he does, including family, business, and taking the time to celebrate success with those that worked hard to make it happen, makes life extraordinary.

John Howie's generous loyalty also isn't reserved just for staff or his home life. Dozens of nonprofit organizations have benefitted from a John Howie Restaurant donation to support nearly every kind of mission. John Howie Restaurants are recognized as one of the most giving businesses in the Puget Sound area. Part of that call to give comes from Chef Howie's dedication to the Golden Rule: *Do unto others as you would have them do unto you.* It's Chef Howie's goal to remember that no matter how much life throws at you, everyone deserves basic respect, honor and care.

CHEF HOWIE'S FAVORITE QUOTES

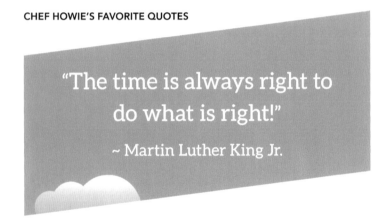

"The time is always right to do what is right!"

~ Martin Luther King Jr.

Chef John Howie

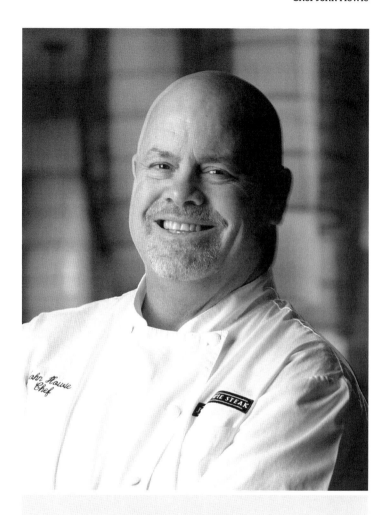

CHEF JOHN HOWIE

Faithful · High Integrity
Extraordinary Work Ethic
Generous · Teachable
Smart · Strong · Discerning
High Standards
Grateful
Inspirational

HEATHER TUININGA

> I only have to spend five minutes with Heather and I'm a better person because she helps bring out the best in everyone she meets and that's extraordinary. ~ L. S.

Blazoned across the top of every $20 bill are the words, *In God We Trust*. These four words best describe Heather Tuininga's belief that a $20 bill can change lives, and she's been given plenty of reasons to think so. On a stage in a local performing arts center thirty minutes east of Seattle, Heather joins several other notable women whom 425 Business Magazine named game changers in the region. Assembled on a long sofa, the women include leaders who have attained success though financial gain, or who've been identified as evangelists for positive lifestyle changes. Heather is there to tell them something they don't always think about when it comes to leading an accomplished life. Some may dismiss her ideas because they think they're only applicable to affluent people with deep pockets. But Heather is about to get everyone in the theater thinking differently, positing that anyone can become a philanthropist, just like her, regardless of income.

As Heather shares examples about how small amounts of money can make a giant difference, the crowd begins to tune into her thinking. Even though she's been in the company of some very wealthy, influential people, she wants this audience of varied means to think about one question: *What difference would $20 make to someone if you gave it away?*

HEATHER'S FAVORITE QUOTES

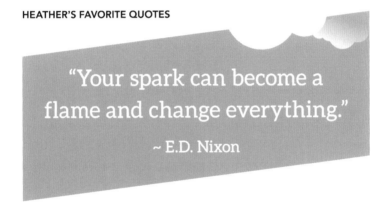

"Your spark can become a flame and change everything."

~ E.D. Nixon

Most people in the room are assuming she's talking about the difference $20 will make to the receiver. However, for Heather, that's just part of her mission. She's a Joy Opportunist, and her consultancy holds giving as part of its core mission. She wants to share with the women in the room what giving can do for the giver's soul. She's learned to find out not only how donors want to make a difference but just as important, why they're compelled to donate to one specific need. She then helps them realize that in some parts of the world, a relatively small amount of money can change an entire village forever. Her mission is to align donors with causes they feel compelled to positively impact and show them how even $20 can make a difference. Having visited some of the most impoverished nations in Africa herself, she knows the places where donors can make an immediate impact. Whether it's a child headed home in Uganda, a school in Rwanda, or clean drinking water in the many parts of the world that have no access to it, Heather confidently links donors to giving paths they can walk. Few donor engagements result in short-term commitments.

The joy that givers experience when they've aligned themselves with a solution that's making a real difference keeps them involved and often attracts others to join. Heather helps people understand how to tap into joy born of giving and when it happens, she also explains why they feel that way. Plenty of studies have brought back conclusive evidence that giving, in any amount, makes people happier. Those who give long-term to causes they deeply care about have a better view of their own life, less stress, and better relationships than those who don't practice regular philanthropic giving. Heather believes generosity changes everything, including lives, family, hopes, dreams, and communities. She's also certain that generosity matters now more than ever. People are longing to make an impact, and because it can be made without immense resources, many more people can now contribute, both in the U.S. and around the world. Heather creates a plan for individuals and families that is called their "Journey of Generosity." It's a path for them that includes plenty of ways to experience the same joy she and her family receive through giving.

Much of Heather's calling to philanthropy was set by example in her early years. Her mother gave freely of her time, kind words, and service to the community. Heather's mom showed her that not all resources are made of dollars and cents. The spirit of giving is a dynamic of sharing what you have, no matter the size or quantity. Her mother's "Journey of Generosity" was founded in happiness, joy, laughter, and welcoming those she'd never met. Following her mother's path, Heather feels those same emotions. She continues her mom's legacy by giving homemade jams and special birthday cakes to others, by opening her home, and by cultivating the same spirit of philanthropy she saw in her mom. Equally, Heather's father exemplified a commitment to high standards, putting others first, especially his family and community, which are commitments Heather continues to carry on in her own life. Her father made it clear that the world Heather was entering was hers for the taking, and with discipline and nonnegotiable high-standards, she would never fall short.

Of greatest importance, Heather's dad always showed up to the sidelines of her sporting events and in the school gym for music recitals. He was always there in his suit and tie. She could always count on him.

Heather is grateful for many things her parents gave her, but especially the gift of knowing acts of service are a way of loving others. She also credits three other special women for showing her a path of faith that, to this day, drives her spiritual journey. Nancy, Rita, and Christine have each shown Heather a love of Jesus that is gentle and full of grace. They have also frequently encouraged her to see beauty and promise in loving herself. This spiritual sisterhood has elevated Heather's ability to reach out to others who need to feel intimate with Christ. This sisterhood has also triumphed over Heather's need to be a super-achiever and instead has encouraged her to be a super-believer. Heather knows it's this group of faithful, generous women that has kept her inspired, humbled, and focused on letting God love her abundantly.

HEATHER'S FAVORITE QUOTES

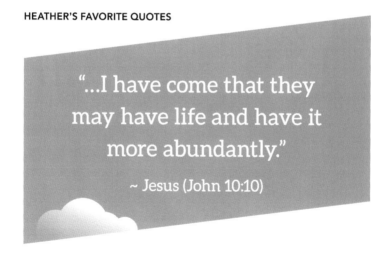

"...I have come that they may have life and have it more abundantly."

~ Jesus (John 10:10)

Above all, she feels her dad's high standards for her and the demonstration of love shown to her by her sisterhood have set her up to give others the "Gift of Generosity" and the joy that comes with it. Between her parents, these three sisters in Christ, and many others Heather has helped, she's discovered several similarities. Primarily, each has freed him or herself from the prison that can come with wealth and accumulation of expensive material possessions that don't create the same joy as does the transformation of people and communities. Heather has never met an unhappy generous person or a former giver.

A form of giving that Heather has seen create lasting joy in her life is when others donate their time, encouragement, patience, love, and resources unconditionally. Her mission is to let that generosity she's experienced flow through her and create a legacy to help others do the same.

Heather feels similarly about her education. The high standards she grew up with at home also showed up in her high school and college writing teachers' instruction. Their generous use of red pens allowed Heather many opportunities to keep improving. Each of them pushed her toward excellence. Today, Heather could not be more grateful for those many late-night rewrites. She acknowledges that, if not for her extensive education – which included political science, economics, and public policy – and the diligence which she practiced because of these disciplined instructors, many of her opportunities simply wouldn't have happened. One of these was being part of a yearlong national education exchange at the University of Massachusetts, Amherst during her junior year. She also had the benefit of living in the northeast, where she formed many lifelong friendships, and ran the Boston Marathon. Also, while earning her master's degree at Duke University, Heather traveled and performed in China with the Duke Chapel Choir. Additionally, her graduate studies garnered her a teaching internship in Toledo, Ohio, from where she still revisits the Duke University college basketball program annually. She experienced all of these opportunities by using her father's high standards as a compass.

In addition to her substantial record of education, along the way Heather has also absorbed some important advice to live by. As an intentional listener, she applies the best life lessons she's seen and heard to her own experience. One of the most important ones was to "put the big rocks in your life first." Taken from a college professor, the practice of filling a jar with the biggest stones representing God, Marriage, Family, and Good Stewardship first, to be followed with the smaller stones in life, while there is still room, greatly impacted her thinking. Heather uses this principle nearly every day when making decisions about how to prioritize her time, resources and thoughts. It keeps her from getting mired in the smallest of details that can burn up a day, a week, or a month, while the best parts of her life stall.

Another wise piece of counsel Heather was gifted was from spiritual confidant, Rita. It came in the form of a question while Heather was trying to muscle some initiatives into action. Not having success at the pace she'd hoped for even though all the pieces seemed ready to assemble, Rita presented Heather with a solution she wishes she'd learned 20 years earlier. As Heather struggled with how to move forward when things just hadn't achieved the momentum they should have had in Heather's high-achiever world, Rita asked, "Wouldn't you rather have God's handprints on this than your own?"

HEATHER'S FAVORITE QUOTES

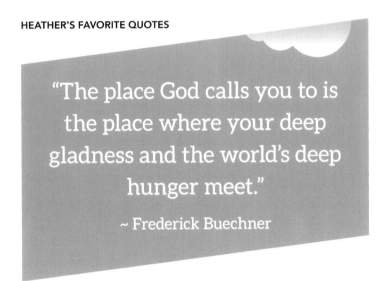

"The place God calls you to is the place where your deep gladness and the world's deep hunger meet."

~ Frederick Buechner

From the moment that question hit Heather's well-versed brain and every day since, Heather has let God take the wheel after she does her diligent, laser-focused preparation. Due to that one timely question, Heather has never understood the word "patience" like she does now. Thanks to Rita, Heather can enter a project or endeavor not necessarily knowing the timeline or if it's even going to produce the intended outcome. Her competitive advantage, though, is the confidence of knowing so long as she does her part well, she can entrust the rest to God.

As Heather helps others understand the benefits of sharing their time and resources, she also asks them to do it without judgment because she knows their joy will return to them tenfold. Heather continues to see this joy of generosity in those who choose to use their time and resources for a greater purpose than they initially intended. Heather is also a firm believer that one small act can begin a movement that will have lasting and real effect on outcomes for others. Her passion for helping entire communities in Africa and other deeply impoverished places in the world is a meaningful opportunity to make a giant difference and get incredible joy and satisfaction watching the progress. Heather has also seen how humility and generosity make a great combination.

Heather isn't the only one in her house that bestows these virtues. Husband, Eric, also sees the benefits of joy as he and Heather impact others with their personal time and resources. In Eric, Heather has been given something for which she waited 36 years. When Heather looks at him, she knows this is the man God designed for her. An advocate for her on every level, Eric provides her a "soft landing strip" when things aren't always right, which can be challenging when you're married to a woman with DNA that includes very high standards. The son of a single mother, Eric is a firm believer in women's strength. His life is also dedicated to God. Heather has a deep appreciation for his excellent communication skills, love of people, outward joy, and gratitude for life. She and Eric have no trouble collectively identifying their "big rocks" and try to always place them in their "jar of life" first.

Five years ago, Heather and Eric received a gift from God when daughter, Kate, was born into their lives. Those who've met Kate see right away that she is a special little girl. With Jesus in her heart, a smile on her beautiful face, and a kind word to all that will listen, Kate leaves every person she meets happy to have met her. She isn't afraid to engage in conversation with passers-by either. Heather has lost count of the times she's been told Kate's brief conversation made a person's day. Eric and Heather are confident Kate's life will be lived with purpose and plenty of God's love in her heart. Heather hopes Kate's faith journey will also be as deeply felt as hers has been.

Although Heather spent plenty of hours in church growing up, she wasn't sure how it applied to her. It wasn't until her teens that she determined true faith wasn't about religion or doctrine. The day Heather realized her relationship with Jesus was personal, everything about faith became clear to her. She would never profess her faith to be exact, in fact just the opposite. Nearly a decade ago Heather began a new walk with God, one that didn't seek perfection or even approval. This path is one that has led Heather to living with the confidence that she is loved by God. That unconditional love blesses her on everything she does, even if it's not perfect or as she designed it.

As Heather looks forward to sharing the message of joyful generosity, she accepts that God will continue to mold her and gently guide her where she needs to go. She's most excited to help others find those one or two issues they can impact.

Heather and Eric give toward villages they support in Africa, as well as important issues on native soil. Both set higher goals every year for their generosity journey, trusting God, and experiencing the joy when the gifts are shared. Mom and Dad know Kate is watching and learning from their every move. In Kate, Heather aims to model her own actions. She wants her daughter to learn high character, a heavy desire to let God love her, and to be someone who completely understands joy in generosity. Kate is Heather and Eric's "joy central." Even at five-years-old, Kate now knows it takes just $20 to create a joyful giver and grateful receiver.

HEATHER TUININGA

You can read inspiring $20 stories at Heather's
website at 1010strategies.com

Smart
Modest · Honest
Caring · Capable

SENATOR ANDY HILL

(1962-2016)

> Few people have created more positive change in government in such a short span, all to benefit those who needed it most. I cannot say enough about Andy's extraordinary contribution to the people of the State of Washington. ~ L. S.

State of Washington Governor Jay Inslee signed Senate Bill 5375, The Andy Hill (CARE) Cancer Research Endowment, into law on January 30, 2018. Dozens of Senator Hill's close friends, the senator's wife, Molly, and some of the brightest minds in medical research surrounded the governor at the signing table. The legislation is Senator Andy Hill's legacy, a bill he worked on himself, that ensures Washington State will continue to attract the top cancer researchers with the aim of finding a therapy that will curb the very disease that took Andy Hill's life in the fall of 2016.

Andy Hill spent four years in office in Olympia. During that time, his stamp of compassion made him a champion for marriage equality, tuition cuts for college students, and protection for those with developmental disabilities including those on the Autism Spectrum.

As Chair of the Ways and Means Committee, Senator Hill took it upon himself to generate the needed support for legislation that would provide long-overdue respite for families with children that require long term, specialized therapies including ABA — Applied Behavior Analysis. This legislative benefit and several others that would fundamentally change the everyday life of the developmentally disabled and their families was shepherded into law by Andy as the Vulnerable Individuals Priority (VIP) Act. Even though he didn't have a direct exposure to the issue of developmental disabilities and the multitude of challenges associated with them, Andy recognized the hundreds of children and adults that this one bill would impact. He was willing to advocate on both sides of the aisle and when the vote for the VIP Act was taken on March 28th, 2014, the Senate tally was 93-0. The newly passed bill provided help for 15,000 families that had been on a waiting list for several years. Andy was showered with praise and accolades by advocacy groups statewide for renewing their faith in a government system that had left them marginalized for decades.

Fighting for position and place started early in life for Andy. His mother, Claudia, instilled a sense of drive and ambition in her second-born son. The tight bond between them included unlimited confidence in Andy's choices around sports and his educational path. Unlike his older brother, who followed closely in his father's footsteps onto the tennis court, Andy felt more himself on the soccer field. His choice to play a team sport provided him cover from having his dad offer too much coaching advice due to his limited understanding of the rules.

ANDY'S FAVORITE QUOTES

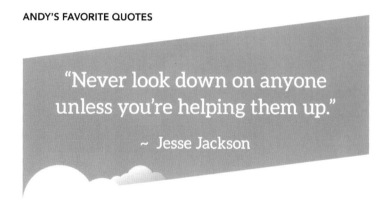

"Never look down on anyone unless you're helping them up."

~ Jesse Jackson

Andy also gained great footing in life being married to Molly. His love for her was giant. Molly will remember Andy for many things but the top of the list includes his humor, intellect, and ability to think of others above himself. She always took comfort in knowing he respected her thoughts, opinions, and decisions. Through multiple career decisions and the calling to run for public office, every life changing transition was made only after a mutual agreement and acknowledgement of the possible outcomes. Molly and the couple's two kids helped Andy become a fantastic father because he knew they believed in him and would support the toughest decisions, including the decision to become a public figure.

One of Andy's biggest professional influences was David Cole, Andy's first boss after he graduated from Harvard business school. Andy's respect for David was immense and fortunately for Andy, David felt the same way about him. David's high expectations brought out the best in Andy, who did not want to disappoint. On more than one occasion, Andy postponed family vacations to meet deadlines. David definitely brought out the best in Andy and rewarded him with added responsibility and authorship.

Throughout his life, personal and professional relationships helped Andy find the best version of himself. Several of those confidants grew close to Andy when the doctor told him he had lung cancer in 2009. Through the treatments and recovery, this tribe stayed near until he was given the all clear a year later. That green light was catalyst for his run for the Washington State Senate. With the encouragement of his closest allies, Andy ran and won the opportunity to get involved with public service at a high level. He saw this office as a way to honor the people of Washington. Throughout his professional life and serving in public office, Andy often would reflect on how his education had elevated his life and had taken him places he hadn't imagined, including the soccer team at a New York college.

A self-admitted under achiever when it came to school, Andy's choices for college were few. Fortunately for Andy, the coach of the Colgate University soccer team spotted his play and recruited him to play goalie. This vote of confidence energized Andy to give more, in both sport and school, than he ever had before. His respect for his teachers also rose to a new level as he came to see each of them as a life changer. He valued their unique abilities to bring out the best in him, the other students, and to tackle problems from several angles. Andy's appreciation of teachers led him to spend much of his adult life helping out in public school classrooms. Andy's gap year between high school and college was dedicated to being an instructional assistant in the Denver public school system. He did the same at the end of his first career, filling in where needed in the public school systems near their family home. Andy believed in the idea that when you teach a man to fish, you give him the tools to care for himself forever. He shared plenty of counsel and advice in the classroom, in his professional life, and during his time in office. Andy was also given plenty of solid guidance that helped determine some of his best moves. While moving his way up the leadership ladder in his first job, post Colgate, Andy determined his Computer Science and Physics degree lacked the needed business skillset to make it to the level to which he aspired. His boss agreed to write Andy a letter of recommendation but with one caveat. Unless Andy was applying at the very best business schools in the country, he preferred Andy stay put. When Harvard's MBA programs came calling, his boss told him he'd be crazy not to attend.

ANDY'S FAVORITE QUOTES

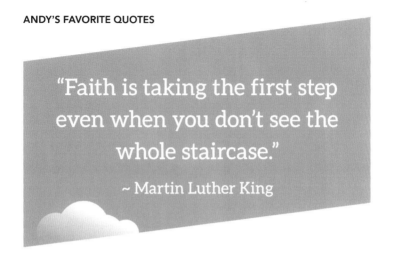

"Faith is taking the first step even when you don't see the whole staircase."

~ Martin Luther King

Another important way finder for Andy – one that Molly shared with the beyond-standing-room-only crowd at his life celebration – was called the "Two Year Rule." Trying to learn from the tough lessons of a divorce, Andy believed, for the benefit of all, it was best to date and get to know a possible future spouse for a minimum of two years. In his mind that same personal mission should apply to having children as well. This combined four-year runway wasn't part of Molly's playbook when they met but looking back she can endorse the plan based on their own outcome.

When asked, Andy always happily shared his thoughts on living an accomplished life. His mantra: *Learn, Earn*, and *Serve* captured what he felt were the three ways to make the most of a fully-actualized life. He also would share some valuable statistics he believed in with anyone who would listen: If you can finish high school, stay away from drugs, and avoid having children before the age of 21, the odds of avoiding poverty greatly improve. These facts Andy had read and shared many times with others guided him as husband and father from the beginning of life with Molly. Introduced by mutual friends just after Andy graduated from business school, he would head west to Seattle. They would see each other every three weeks during their New York-Seattle courtship that lasted exactly two years. As per the plan, the first of three children came two years later. Much like dad, each of the kids took to the soccer field. They also loved exploring mountain trails together, learning to ski as a family, sitting around the fire while camping, and traveling when the time was right. Andy depended on Molly as CEO of the house while he worked his way through various leadership posts at Microsoft. His office schedule, regular community forums, campaign events, and business travel kept Molly on the run with three kids and a home to manage. A consequence of being in office was living in Olympia and only visiting home on weekends during the legislative session. Molly believes that although this was a true sacrifice for the family, it was a worthy one because, as she reminisces back to the difference Andy was making, the time was well invested in the lives of those who needed him most.

Remembering Andy is a constant for Molly because each of her children clearly resembles him. On a regular basis, comments about the similarities come from family and friends. Each of the kids finds this an honor to their fantastic dad.

Strength to battle alongside Andy through two rounds of cancer took immense faith. Andy was raised in the Episcopal Church and Molly from a succession of Irish Catholics. Not long after meeting her, Andy could see part of his two year plan with Molly was going to include a return to church. With the help of Father Tim Clark of their local parish, Andy and family aimed to live out the Gospel rather than simply attend Mass. A gifted and well-read priest, Father Tim helped Andy re-discover the faith he had once known. Even after Father Tim was transferred to another parish community, he and Andy always kept in touch. Molly received word that during Andy's health challenges, Father Tim would ask his new parish to lift up Andy in their prayers. Molly and Andy decided to make the trip to his parish knowing his sermons would add energy and spirit to Andy's fight. Father Tim made several visits to the Hill home in the closing days of Andy's life. Molly could sense the peace in Andy's weak demeanor each time Father Tim was near him. Father Tim made it a point to be near Andy shortly after he died. Molly believes Andy passed in peace.

Andy will always be remembered as a man not afraid to get involved, be it in the schools volunteering with highly capable math students, keeping track of the funds for PTSA, or leading one of the most dynamic soccer leagues in the state. When he saw the need, Andy didn't steer away from the tough community projects around him. When the youth soccer association he led wanted to develop more playing fields but the current use was a competing interest, Andy brought the stakeholders together over several meetings and helped craft a mutually agreeable plan. It was during these contentions negotiations that Andy was noticed as the calm catalyst in the room. Government officials saw a future legislator in Andy. They believed his calm demeanor and wisdom would go a long way in state government.

Molly believes Andy's legacy will continue to inspire others in the areas that mattered most to him. Of late, few in elected office have been able to reach across the aisle in an honest effort to represent all interests like Andy did. His need to make sure all voices had a chance to be heard was a quality everyone could agree on. After Andy's passing, Molly received stacks of letters from legislators, stakeholders, and ordinary citizens about how Andy made a real effort to understand their side of an issue. It gives Molly great joy to know she was the wife of a man that had an impact on so many people. Andy still walks beside Molly as she goes out in the world every day. It's the world he made much better for her, his three children and all six million people in the Evergreen State.

SENATOR ANDY HILL

SENATOR ANDY HILL AND MOLLY HILL

Thank you Molly for supplying meaningful
information for Andy's profile.

**Resilient
Tenacious · Intuitive
Compassionate
Open-minded**

ARZU FOROUGH

My gratitude overflows when I think about how one woman with a mission created a cause that now stands beside 2,000 families with autistic children. Arzu and her team provide extraordinary resources to those who have few places to turn for answers. ~ L. S.

Sitting in the busy waiting room of a multi-doctor pediatrician's office, a young couple waits expectantly. They're a bundle of nerves. After the third call from their seven-year-old son Bryce's school about his not being able to get through the school day without a classroom altercation and subsequent trip to see the principal, both parents agree it's time to get some real answers. Earlier analysis had tagged their child with a slight learning deficit. Mom and dad were both led to believe that a mainstream school experience would be the right way for their only child to catch up with his peers. Since preschool, Bryce had struggled with social situations and, as a result, been invited to fewer birthday parties and playdates. Electronics have become the safest and most engaging way to keep him content.

A young nurse comes through door and calls Bryce's

name. Trudging down the hallway, Bryce enters the pediatrician's office with his parents. She smiles warmly at them. After a brief conversation, she asks Bryce's parents if they're comfortable with Bryce sitting in the waiting room alone, so the adults can have a private conversation. They comply. Comfortably seated with a gaming tablet in his hands, Bryce will be fine. As the compassionate doctor begins talking by using plenty of medical speak that makes no sense to the technology couple, she tells them her assessment is that Bryce needs to see a doctor who can do a full screening for something she refers to as a "spectrum disorder."

The couple may not be trained in medicine, but they've done a lot of reading while trying their best to be advocates and loving parents. Those two words made them sit back a little further in their seats. The father cuts to the chase and asks the doctor if she believes Bryce has autism. Not being a specialist in the field but having seen plenty of kids his age with nearly the same social behavior, she tells them yes, that she does believe a referral to Seattle Children's Autism Center is in order.

In the parents' eyes, this conversation is finished. They'd like to gather their things and go. But the doctor believes one more visit with Bryce is in her patient's best interest, especially since his parents are about to walk out with even more mental baggage than they had when they arrived. The doctor knows there is plenty of love in this family and she wants to keep it that way. Continuing the conversation, she shares with Bryce that she has a couple of doctor friends who can help him have more fun at school, a need she picked up in her brief conversation with him.

On their long car ride home, the family is quiet. Once home, while Bryce sits in his normal spot with a gaming remote, mom and dad sit in front of a different monitor doing what most would do with this news, researching the Internet for topics on autism. Above wanting to know more about autism and other spectrum disorder terms, what they really hope to find is someone who's not in the medical world who can calm their fears. As they search for autism therapy services and several other keywords, one name keeps coming up: Arzu Forough, founder of Washington Autism Alliance and Advocacy (WAAA) in Redmond, Washington. Searching for organizations that offer related services to families of autistic children, that same name appears. Like any parent facing a medical diagnosis involving their child, they continue to look anywhere they can to find answers.

Even though the World Wide Web can make the possibility of finding a nearby solution impossible, the solid information they need is under ten miles from home. After their first conversation with Arzu, Bryce's parents begin to feel the tension in their shoulders relax and the pit in their stomachs loosen. It is clear Arzu understands what they're experiencing. She shares her unique journey of having two children on the spectrum and the struggle to get them the individualized help they needed. Bryce's parents begin to realize, like nearly 3,000 other families in Washington State, that Arzu and her team at WAAA will be the key to a new normal in their quest to be a family.

Bryce's story represents a similar path to nearly every case for which WAAA goes to battle. Health insurance companies are not keen on standing with autism families for many reasons, the primary being economic. Depending on the diagnosis with respect to where they fit on the Autism Spectrum Disorder (ASD) the child may need as many as 25 hours a week of specialized help, on top of school hours. The duration can be as long as six years. This scenario is the type of claim that insurance companies and their shareholders don't want under any circumstances.

While living in Texas, Arzu's own journey trying to reason with insurance companies that denied claims for her own two young children was the genesis of her advocacy. Like Bryce's parents, Arzu reached out to the world and found that support for parents was minimal at best. What she did find, though, were a lot of parents in a similar fight trying to get healthcare insurance companies to include any coverage for their children with an autism diagnosis. Being a fierce advocate for her children's future, Arzu took on the insurance system in the Lone Star state. Arzu's two sons were the first children in Texas to receive Applied Behavior Analysis (ABA) coverage by private insurance. Another relief came to Arzu's family when her older son was the first child in the state to qualify for the Medically Dependent Child Program. Each of these victories took an immense effort fighting a very steep uphill battle. This was a giant development for other families as, prior to Arzu's outcome, children did not qualify for any developmental services past age three.

ARZU'S FAVORITE QUOTES

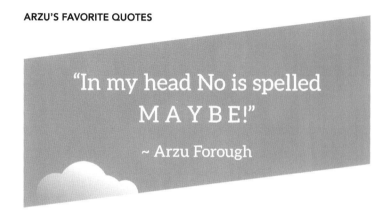

"In my head No is spelled M A Y B E!"

~ Arzu Forough

Arzu credits her eldest aunt for giving her the drive to move through difficult circumstances to a positive result. When she was just five-years-old, Arzu's father left their native Iran to study in the United States. Joining her aunt who already had nine children in her care, Arzu was too young to understand they were living in desperate poverty. Even living in these tough conditions, Arzu remembers those years as being some of her best childhood memories. Her aunt's limitless energy, optimism, and laughter helped keep a very crowded home moving in the right direction. Arzu's husband is also an added source of strength for her. Throughout all the battles and challenges, he's the one that reminds Arzu when she needs to add more patience and perseverance. Her husband is also the one who provided the green light to move to Seattle when it became clear that the best work for ABA was being done at University of Washington Autism Center. When a leadership position opened for him at the University of Washington (UW), Arzu and her family made the journey to the Pacific Northwest. Arzu was disappointed that although the meaningful work at UW was creating the desired result for families with autistic children, her husband's new health insurance package did not cover autism therapy treatment. Like she did in Texas, Arzu worked again to initiate change. She founded Washington Autism Alliance and Advocacy and before she knew it, the grassroots organization was carrying the flag for 1,000 families in Washington state.

Arzu believed a state as progressive as Washington needed to recognize autism as a developmental issue that had to be covered in statewide health insurance policies. She began making two-hour daily trips to the state capital in Olympia to get her mission in front of legislators who could enact change. At that time, only Microsoft had specific language in their benefits package that covered lengthy ABA for dependent children. Arzu began her efforts in Olympia by meeting with every single legislator about insurance reform. Through that process, she and her team realized that all the legislative change and protection they sought was already written into law. Her exhaustive work in Olympia gave her confidence that the bill her team helped author would create the path for insurance coverage which thousands of families desperately needed. The Combating Autism Act included the specific language Arzu believed would open coverage access for families. Her timing of trying to push this bill through the needed committees couldn't have been worse. In the depths of a recession, the leaders in Olympia were spending most of their time try to solve a massive operating budget loss.

Arzu's fight was far from over. Combing over existing laws with the help of legal advocates, she realized much of the language to protect children with autism and developmental disabilities was already in place. The lawmakers had just been remiss implementing and funding them. There also seemed to be lack of motivation to do so. To combat this apathy, Arzu formed a legal partnership to represent WAAA. She filed several class action lawsuits to clarify existing laws and ensure insurance companies would be held accountable for the coverage of medically necessary screening, diagnosis and treatment of autism and other developmental disabilities. These legal maneuvers created action among lawmakers, prompting insurers in the state of Washington to be responsible.

WAAA can measure its effectiveness in several ways. Eleven years ago, when Arzu began her quest to gain coverage for her two sons, just one employer offered comprehensive healthcare insurance that included ABA and individualized educational plans. Today, Arzu and her dedicated staff help more than 3,000 families throughout Washington state navigate their current coverage options.

Arzu's *Individualized Education Program* supplement and teachers' guidelines became a requirement for all teachers working with learners with autism spectrum disorders statewide in 2008.

Even with these wins, Arzu is concerned about a specific set of families she is unable to meaningfully serve. An entire population of low-income families has zero access to the same treatment as those who benefit from employer-paid healthcare insurance. These same families aren't able to navigate the public education system. WAAA does its very best to guide each low-income family, but without the benefit of all the medical services the family needs, especially individualized education planning, the results are often not positive.

ARZU'S FAVORITE QUOTES

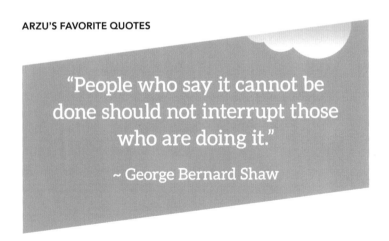

"People who say it cannot be done should not interrupt those who are doing it."

~ George Bernard Shaw

Arzu has relied on both her formal education and years of continuing education in her work. It wasn't her original intention to start an advocacy organization. But between extended learning in nonprofit administration, intervention education, and shaping public policy, she acquired the needed tools to do so. Arzu also understands and advocates for neurodiversity, developmental disabilities, and autism screening. Additionally, some of the best training she's received has come from the advice of others, including her beloved late grandmother. Part of Arzu's passion for making sure schools accept their responsibility to educate children no matter what their ability is to learn came from her grandmother's statement, "it's not your children's responsibility to serve their schools, it's their school's responsibility to serve your children!" Through the words of others, Arzu has also determined that so long as she focuses on a life well-lived through generosity, compassion, and integrity, her time serving others is well spent.

Arzu's faith has played an important role in shaping her impassioned life. Much of how she puts her faith in action is by allowing it to be her inner voice and moral compass. Arzu has also benefitted by trying to concentrate on small incremental goals in building WAAA and in her role as mother and wife. Keeping her eye on short-term benchmarks has allowed her to stay on track when others facing her daunting objectives might give up. Much of the support to keep pressing forward comes from the families she serves. As WAAA grew, Arzu realized her work was becoming much more than a group of concerned parents. The movement quickly grew to thousands of families and she began to realize just how many unrepresented families like her own needed WAAA. Arzu quickly realized that because being heard is often accomplished by scale, an alignment with other community organizations would enable her to build a stable, stronger and much more sustainable network. This statewide collaboration has become the advocacy network Arzu now leans on when her phone rings from someone calling her from 300 miles away.

ARZU'S FAVORITE QUOTES

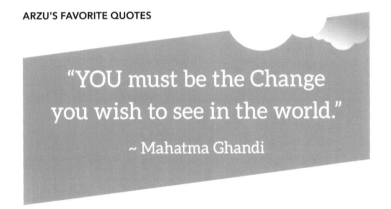

> "YOU must be the Change you wish to see in the world."
>
> ~ Mahatma Ghandi

These partnerships have also allowed her to concentrate on the future. She sees a giant, unmet need among the generation of young adults like her two sons. Their lifelong learning needs and ability to stay safe in their future communities is why Arzu believes she needs to invest in this next wave of services. The current level of long-term residential housing for autistic and developmentally disabled in the state is minimal. Children like Bryce will need a path for a safe and successful adulthood. That work is still to be done. But for now, Bryce's parents know Arzu Forough, that name that kept coming up as they desperately tried to find answers for little Bryce. Bryce's parents, and thousands of others, now know Arzu has their back.

ARZU FOROUGH

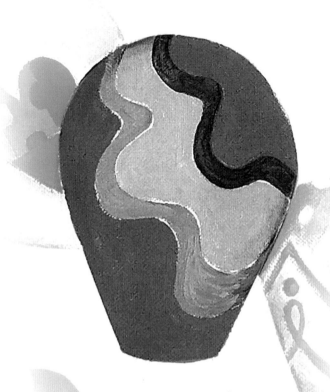

Driven · Caring
Creative · Excitable
Decisive · Integrity
Inspirational
Accountable

BARRY HORN

I'm grateful to have watched Barry scale a company and build an extraordinary foundation that focuses on aligning businesses with nonprofit organizations. Thousands of youth, near and far, benefit from the work that started as a way for employees to share their time and earnings. ~ L. S.

In a capacity Bellevue, Washington conference room with 75 chairs facing forward, an eager group waits to hear tales of a one-week voyage to Batzchocolá, Guatemala. Few, if any, of the ten people who made this brave journey had ever been to a developing country prior to going, much less one fresh out of a devastating civil war. Complete with photos to document the adventurous week, Liberty Financial CEO, Barry Horn, starts by saying, "This was the most dangerous thing I've ever done in my life." He then shares about people in need, how his heart grew exponentially in the jungle of Central America, and how his company made a large promise that he intends to keep.

Barry didn't have to make this trip. His financial services company of 100 employees had plenty of hands in the air when this idea was floated as a way of giving back to the community. What sets Barry apart from others that support causes with gifts to create serious and meaningful change is that he needed to see firsthand what he was being asked to support. What Barry saw in Guatemala was an opportunity to rally his people to make a giant difference in the lives of 61 families that fled into the woods when their village was burned to the ground. After the Liberty group's initial journey, Agros International, the Seattle-based international aid and economic facilitation organization, helped Barry's team stay regularly connected through field reports and photos, showing how the company's resources were literally rebuilding life in Batzchocolá one building and one coffee plant at a time.

With Barry staying stateside, subsequent travel to the village by passionate Liberty employees had the same effect on everyone. A major development, made in part by Liberty employees, was the building of a basic road to replace a narrow trail. This was a game changer for getting supplies in and crops out to market. That project became the namesake of today's renowned Liberty Road Foundation. Within just a few years, the people of this completely remote village in the hills of Guatemala had a working village, coffee crops to export, and deep gratitude for this group of faraway visitors that had given them an opportunity to return to their native land.

Barry began to imagine how many other places, preferably closer to home, could benefit from the enthusiasm he and his team had for lifting and supporting others. As the foundation continued to grow, especially in fundraising, a remarkable couple was brought on to add stability and effect to the organization. For more than a decade, Dr. John and Karilyn Dammerell have been guiding the day-to-day operation of Liberty Road Foundation. With John filling the role of Executive Director and Karilyn providing operations support, in a short period of time LRF has been able to grow substantially. From one nonprofit beneficiary in Guatemala, to six a decade later, LRF is impacting local communities that serve street ministries, addiction recovery, foster children, human trafficking, equine therapy, and marginalized youth. Barry knows each of these causes very well because he's seen with his own two eyes the difference generosity has made for them.

BARRY'S FAVORITE QUOTES

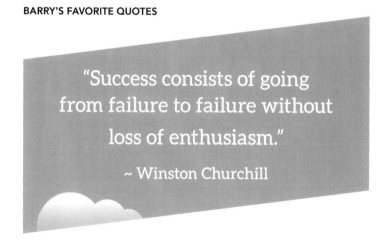

"Success consists of going from failure to failure without loss of enthusiasm."

~ Winston Churchill

More than the financial growth, Liberty Road Foundation (LRF) has expanded its network of passionate supporters to include other business partners. This innovative way of enabling other small businesses to join the LRF mission has been a key to its growth. Rarely does a small business have the opportunity to be part of a hands-on foundation doing excellent, life-changing work in a major metro market like Seattle and the communities that surround it. This business partner network provides that opportunity and also creates a group of like-minded thinkers when it comes to fundraising and spreading the message of LRF to a wider audience. This is also where Barry finds the excitement in his vision of LRF.

Barry's love of convening community and business was seeded at his Uncle's Mercedes Benz dealership. Spending nearly all his spare time among the German luxury cars, Barry gained appreciation for how Uncle Dick ran his business and could see his uncle was representing something he valued and believed in. This set of qualities set a course for Barry's accomplished business career that has included leadership posts in technology and financial services. Another important formative influence on Barry's life was a family friend, Verne Westburg. As a Boeing engineer and father of five, Verne spent his time leading his church community and investing in those around him. Verne became the model Barry would use to form his own path to a life well lived. Also, an early manager at IBM set Barry's direction in business. Not a day passes that Barry isn't practicing the principals imparted to him by his first leader, Dick Radloff. Beyond taking Barry under his wing, Dick set an example of succeeding with integrity and a patient belief in a positive outcome. The lessons of these three men emulate Barry's biggest influence. Jesus has been Barry's moral compass for nearly his entire life. In business, life and community, Jesus continues to be Barry's inspiration and wayfinder.

Learning is a passion Barry developed at Taylor College. Forty years later after graduation, he hasn't stopped learning. He's convinced that consistent daily learning renews his mind, feeding it with a regular diet of positive thoughts and new ideas from current subject matter experts as well as those whose concepts have stood the test of time. His daily journey of ongoing education is also an opportunity to fill his heart with Godly thoughts that renew his gratitude for a blessed life.

Barry's love of family is rooted in his faith. Jesus is the example he follows. Barry wants to love, live and do life in his honor. It's Barry's belief that Jesus has given him extra abilities and resources to reach higher in his business and family life. As Barry puts it, he believes that he does the natural and Jesus does the supernatural.

The study of human behavior fills a part of Barry's days. A piece of advice he was given long ago was the genesis for this interest. Barry is often looking for signs that demonstrate one's character. He believes if he focuses on what people do and not necessarily what they say, that will reveal the most about them. Barry uses this measurement for his own accountability as well. Secondly, he is a true believer that a highly disciplined life leads to more freedom. As Barry observes his own habits, he attributes much of his freedom to enjoy the things he loves most to a set of everyday disciplines, the same three consistent qualities that he sees in his top performers. At the top of that list are those who always exceed and do much more than is required. His goal has always been to set an example and be the type of person who always goes above and beyond. A second consistent practice to being extraordinary is forgiveness. Like Jesus, Barry believes if we keep from holding grudges for wrong doing and simply press on, our minds will be available for the next set of opportunities. He believes a downside to holding out on forgiveness is the long-term destruction of one's health and business. One other practice Barry believes sets high achievers apart is being an early riser.

Setting a daily, written agenda and avoiding the trap of other people's situations that affect your ability to get things accomplished is how Barry lives, every day. At Barry's side for the past fifty years is his wife and very best friend, Joan. Barry gives thanks every day that Joan, his college sweetheart, continues to support him in everything he does. Like Barry, Joan is fond of time with friends in the snow, sun and on the golf course. Joan has also played an active role in organizing and evangelizing the fundraising activities of Liberty Road Foundation. A source of pride and joy for Barry and Joan are their three grandchildren, brought into the world by their daughter, Julie, and her husband, Jack. Family time together provides some of their best lifetime memories. Barry's acumen for success in life and business has also found its way to the next generation. Julie led an accomplished career in information technology before creating a life coach practice to assist those aiming for higher goals in personal and professional development.

Barry's heart and mind have been the beneficiaries of journaling and setting attainable goals. Through optimistic self-talk, his practice of putting goals into writing has directed his mind in a positive direction. He avoids being dragged into negative conversations or habits mainly because that's not the way his mind operates, and they just lead to places he's not headed. One of the many benefits of Liberty Road Foundation is how many can-do, confident, and selfless others like himself have been brought to one organization. Barry thinks because we all live in communities, it's our responsibility to serve each other. Being able to reach into those populations that need help is the function of Liberty Road Foundation. It also exists to attract local businesses looking for a meaningful mission to support.

Because he's earned such abundant blessings, Barry sees it as his personal responsibility to care for those less fortunate than himself. He also views those who need help as equals and hopes the work of his foundation can help steer their lives in a better direction. Looking forward,

Barry doesn't see his road traveling the same path as those in his age bracket. As a focused student of life, he feels he still has much more room to grow, many more people to positively help in business and many more opportunities to find for the Liberty Road Foundation. His desire to stay relevant during changing times through daily learning completely motivates and prepares him for whatever opportunities he encounters.

BARRY'S FAVORITE QUOTES

> "You have enemies? Good, that means you have stood up for something, sometime in your life."
>
> ~ Winston Churchill

Liberty Road Foundation's position at the intersection between nonprofit, business, and philanthropy is what sets it apart from other organizations. Barry's vision of a community that supports itself and each other is alive and well at this crossroad. His desire to demonstrate a well-earned business acumen, rally business partners, lift people out of tough situations, and gain meaningful financial support from trusting donors is Barry's complete picture.

Liberty Road Foundation is hardly a charity. It's a movement where everyone has an opportunity to share their time, talent, or treasure for the betterment of themselves, their community, and some well-deserving non-profit partners. Little did Barry Horn know when he agreed to stake his own life for 61 families in Batzchocolá, Guatemala that it would lead to him creating a cause to care for thousands more on his own native soil.

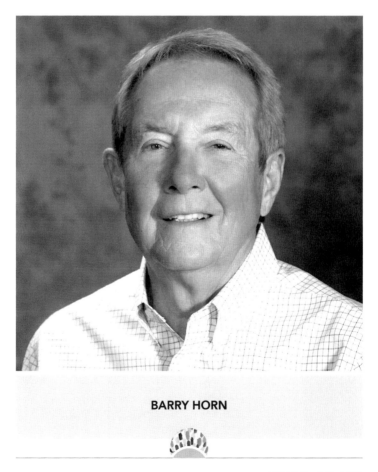

BARRY HORN

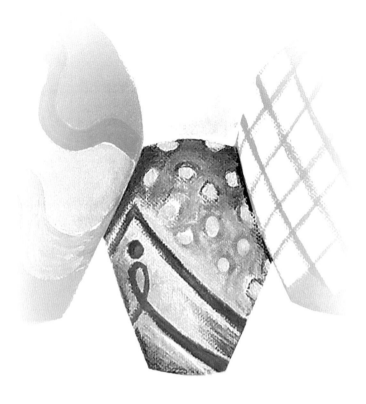

Hospitality
Organized · Goal-oriented
Intentional
Grace and Truth
Gratitude

MARTY HARTMAN

I have faith that unsheltered families, especially single moms, will have a place to sleep because of Marty's extraordinary leadership at Mary's Place. Her team is dedicated to making sure no child ever sleeps outside. ~ L. S.

It's 8:00 AM and the round tables at Mary's Place day shelter in Seattle begin to fill with hungry women, some of them still warming themselves from another night of sleeping outside. A young mom pushes her eight-month-old baby across the floor in a pre-owned stroller the shelter provided for her. She's out of diapers and formula. She's grateful to know this safety net exists but has no desire to make it a long-term solution. Afraid something might happen to her baby during the night, she's had only a few hours of sleep. Ten days ago, after a lengthy night of drinking, her boyfriend, the father of her little girl, threatened her life for the third time. Once he finally passed out, she gathered what she was able to carry and left, never looking back or planning to return.

Visiting friends, asking for a few nights to rest and find

resources to enter emergency housing, she could feel the angry father closing in. Sleeping in her car and moving locations every night became her norm. Once a week, she checked into low-cost, shabby motels to regroup, do laundry, and get a few hours of restless sleep. The support she thought friends and some family would provide seemed to favor the boyfriend. The late-20s mom could do nothing but fend for herself and her child. Within a short time, her funds ran dry and her car was impounded while she was out searching for help. The small bag on the back of the stroller contained her entire life. Feeding her baby with one hand and enjoying a warm breakfast with the other, the young woman felt a hand on her shoulder while she sat at the round table. Mary's Place Executive Director and Head Angel, Marty Hartman, sat with her like she had with hundreds of other domestic violence victims in the past decade. As the leader of Seattle's primary resource for homeless families, Marty and her impassioned team are trying to manage a tsunami of need.

Between the economic boom driven by technology companies, opportunistic residential landlords, and Seattle being the number four opioid-distribution market in the United States, Marty is using every resource imaginable to make sure no child ever sleeps outside. Even with her best efforts, the phone keeps ringing with another family that wants to end sleeping in their car and come inside. Mary's Place has been able to create housing in former office buildings, church basements, surplus county buildings, and a former motel. Marty listens to the emotional young mom explain that she had no idea how hard it would be to live without her abusive boyfriend, but she also couldn't predict when his level of violence would kill her. Fortunately, on this chilly mid-morning, Marty will deliver a miracle like she does for countless young women and families seeking a roof over their heads, if even for a short time. The average wait for families to enter emergency housing in King County is 186 days. This half-year waiting list is part of the reason why visitors to Seattle are stunned that this beautiful, world-class city hosts hundreds of tents, broken-down cars, and RVs. Marty is emphatic that she cannot speak for the actions of the parents, but if there are kids living in these conditions, she's going to find a way to get them off the streets. Through the area-wide network of shelters in King County, Mary's Place has 700 beds for those who are ready to come inside. Although every person living outside is one too many, Marty's priority is families with children. When she delivers the miraculous news to this young woman that she and her child have spent their final night outside, the young woman's tears flow happily. Marty's housing resource team has found a warm and safe shelter where this young mother can at least have the chance to regroup. This reality is Marty's mission at work. For the past two decades, one by one, Marty has led teams that provide a lifeline to people ready to come in and start a better path for themselves.

Marty's mother and father are the genesis of her

compassionate approach to fellow humans. Being the fourth of six children, Marty learned the strength of a family comes from within. Her father was a Major League Baseball relief pitcher, which meant a move every year, a new Catholic school every year, and months of not seeing him during the season. Much of Marty's need to drive solutions and handle situations with grace came from her father. During his absence, Marty and each of her siblings would get phone time talking long distance with him. Even with the miles between them, Marty felt loved and learned the value of communication, even if through a phone line sharing their weekly updates. Spring Training was one time of year they could all be together. Marty recalls countless cross-country road trips with her siblings and the dog, just so they could share that time as a family. In addition to the phone, Marty's mom was fond of letter writing which helped them stay in touch and connected as husband and wife. Marty took many lessons from her father that still help sustain her when the weight of Seattle's homeless crisis gets too heavy. The demand for his services as a standout MLB relief pitcher was built on three key ingredients that Marty takes to Mary's Place every morning. This first is work ethic, followed by always speaking the truth, no matter how difficult the situation.

Marty and her team manage some of the most challenging human conditions possible. The combination of domestic violence, race discrimination, financial ruin, drug addiction, fractured families and mental health challenges leaves Marty no room for anything but truth in her approach to helping each guest at Mary's Place.

MARTY'S FAVORITE QUOTES

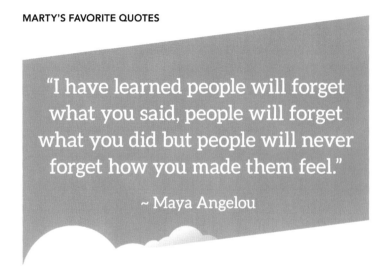

"I have learned people will forget what you said, people will forget what you did but people will never forget how you made them feel."

~ Maya Angelou

The third key ingredient Marty received from her father, and this one from her mother too, was a spirit that spends less time complaining and much more time looking for the solution to problems. Solutions are the equity Marty and her team spend every day at Mary's Place. Whether it's a bus pass, a dozen diapers, a no-cost haircut or a pair of properly fitting shoes, Marty's team uses every moment finding solutions. Agency partners that support Mary's Place number in the dozens, each one of them making their contribution, be it food donations, medical checkups, job skills training, or counseling. Each agency relationship is part of the overall solution at Mary's Place and Marty knows without them, the system of care simply would not work. The families that benefit from these services are the ones that have taught Marty her most valuable lessons. One of these is about faith. More than one mother seeking help from Mary's Place has given Marty these words: *People can take away your belongings, your home, and even your children, but they cannot take away your faith.* Marty uses that lesson every day, and although her work is often very hard, she's never let go of that message.

Marty acknowledges this work is hard but very much worth it. Her husband of 35 years, Dan, has helped instill that fortitude in her. The lesson of working through difficulties, like any average day at Mary's Place, has taught Marty that there is no greater love. Marty has leaned on Dan during the tough days of parenting and getting the foundational pieces of Mary's Place in order. One of those components, and the most important reminder Marty leads her staff with, is the commandment to love your neighbor as yourself. Marty knows that when people are loved they begin to see truth and confidence in relationships. She also knows when people receive love they are far more open to share it with others. Mary's Place was founded on this principal and it has a place in every decision, big and small.

Marty gives credit to her education for seeing Mary's Place to its current scope. Being able to scale a nonprofit when the need is facing nearly epidemic levels takes skill, keen leadership, and a committed Board of Directors. Marty's Catholic-school upbringing brought her a loving relationship with God. It also showed her the many good facets of humanity. The education she took from being a mom was self-control, boundaries, and unconditional love. But the education she uses the most comes from the women and families she serves every day. Marty has needed to take inventory of her own prejudices and biases to impact her families at the highest level.

MARTY'S FAVORITE QUOTES

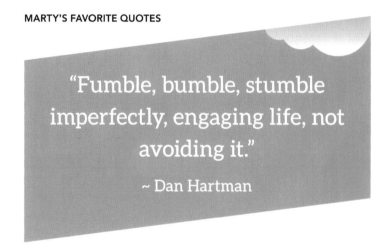

"Fumble, bumble, stumble imperfectly, engaging life, not avoiding it."

~ Dan Hartman

Marty admits her own preconceived thoughts influence her work both positively and negatively. Throughout her journey trying to put Mary's Place on solid ground, many offered advice on how to serve Seattle's unsheltered families. Although the challenge wasn't what it is now, the supply of housing has never met demand. Through this, Marty knows she must just keep trying and never quit, an important educational value her mother passed along when Marty was early in her career. Marty had shown up for the orientation of a newly-landed position in a hospital for profoundly disabled children. The ten new hires shrank to three after the first break. After the lunch break, Marty was the only one remaining. Marty called her mom and said that she wanted to leave too, thinking this was not the job for her. Marty's mom responded, "Give it two weeks," which has been an important set of words Marty has used many times since. She spent two transformative years at that hospital which paid part of her college expenses and created some significant relationships because Marty had to operate far outside her comfort zone. Marty has been able to share this advice and much more with her own four children and grandchildren. With medical providers, a bio-chemist and legal professionals in the family, Marty feels like she and her husband created a household heavy on compassion and learning. Each of Marty's children has spent countless volunteer hours at Mary's Place. Each of them has also adopted much of what Marty learned in her youth (short of having to move all the time) including acknowledging that your neighbor is as important as you. This was one of the first benefits young Marty acquired at Catholic school.

Marty has relied on her faith by asking the community to come beside Mary's Place in a time of specific need. When Mary's Place went to the public with the "No Child Sleeps Outside" goal, her leap of faith was to believe that funding would be contributed at the level needed to expand the shelter capacity. Marty's written goals and prayers were realized, which meant Mary's Place could bring these families in and start trying to resolve their individual housing needs. Realizing this leap of faith informed the community with a specific way to respond and become part of a solution. Those that came forward included faith communities, schools, universities, and neighbors each doing their part to make sure not one child was sleeping outside. Marty also created productive funding alliances with companies that gave employees and customers a way to participate in the campaign that is aimed at bringing every child and family inside.

MARTY'S FAVORITE QUOTES

"Being unwanted, unloved, uncared for, forgotten by everybody – I think that is a much greater hunger, much greater poverty, than the person who has nothing to eat."

~ Mother Teresa

Looking forward, Marty knows there will be more children sleeping outside. Her team will spend every ounce of energy to find them, connect with them, and welcome them in out of the cold.

MARTY HARTMAN

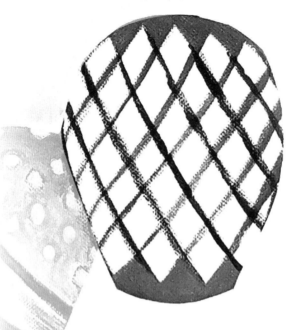

Caring
Creative · Inspiring
Brave · Generous
Passionate

JOHN CHRISTIANSON

I'm inspired that John is able to help others view wealth and time as equal, especially as it pertains to serving others in an extraordinary quest to live fully. ~ L. S.

U nderneath the Spokane Street bridge in Seattle, dozens of high-mileage RVs in various states of disrepair have come to rest. Without any other public property to host them, the City of Seattle has allowed this patchwork of humanity to assemble and live under impossible conditions beneath the four-lane, one-mile, east-west stretch of freeway. Strewn between the RVs are tents of every size, remnants of previous homeless encampments and immense piles of debris. This is the place where John Christianson makes it his mission to visit and share his love with those who may have forgotten what love feels like.

On this chilly 30-degree night, John, wife Kelle, and twenty others, many of whom have never before met, assemble in the basement of a 100-year-old brick mission building in a downtown area of Seattle once known as skid row. Union Gospel Mission Rescue Van leader and former addict, Richard, provides a calming but intentional

15-minute safety overview detailing how each of the three vans will traverse a section of city to distribute supplies to those in need. In addition to a volunteer driver and a steward who spends his day in the recovery program, nine volunteers ride in each red van. Leaving the mission just after 8:00 PM, each group will visit a dozen stops, all in locations that have no resemblance to a standard residential area. Seeing it as a way to truly serve those who need it most, John, Kelle and the ride-along-guests exit their vans under the noisy bridge. As instructed during the safety meeting, each trio walks among the tents, RVs, and shelters created from discarded debris, trying to shout above the street noise to announce that the van has arrived with "blankets, sandwiches, hot chocolate, socks...."

JOHN'S FAVORITE QUOTES

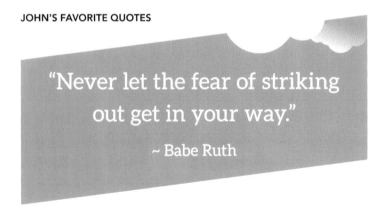

"Never let the fear of striking out get in your way."

~ Babe Ruth

This mandatory self-identification system is an important safety measure to keep volunteers and street residents calm. John is often the first to lead volunteers around the perimeter of an encampment, accepting as much interaction with the people who live there as they'll give him. Through these late-night visits, John and Kelle's encouragement of others has been twofold. With one hand, they reach out to help those on the street. With the other, they guide fearful first-time volunteers (who naturally hold back when approaching an environment that is foreign to them) into dark corridors they would have never otherwise visited.

John is the Founder and CEO of Highland®, where he guides and stewards the wealth and aspirations of some of the most successful people in the country. He specializes in taking a thoughtful approach to integrating life and money, something he calls Living Fully™. Host of *The Wealth Confidant* podcast, available on iTunes, SoundCloud, Overcast & Stitcher, John also writes regularly for *The Wealth Clarity* blog, LinkedIn and has been featured in the *Harvard Business Review*. His hands-on contribution to Seattle's burgeoning homeless population is merely one half of the way he works to be part of the solution to this problem. His active wealth management practice recommends clients invest in organizations like Union Gospel Mission as part of their annual philanthropic giving. John wants his clients and employees to see that giving and serving are equal but, when combined, the sense of money and time well-spent becomes greater. John believes that generosity is a little-known catalyst for joy. Regardless of the size of gift, the act of regular giving makes people happier.

Much of John's passion to lead with a heavy dose of love comes from the roof he grew up under and the one that he sleeps under now. His father gave John the tools to create his own destiny, including leading others to serve in the least likely places. Between persistence and the competitive need to be good at whatever task was before him, John rarely does anything halfway, including his service to others in need.

Equally, his marriage for over 30 years to his wife, Kelle, is an unmitigated journey through courage, change, and personal achievement. John has been both beneficiary and partner on this path. He's completely convinced that joy and giving are two of the best words he can share with others, and has learned this firsthand at home with Kelle, experiencing significant joy by giving to and serving her. Kelle has been the driver of getting their three grown children out into successful married life and she's somehow managed to keep them all on the west coast. Both John and Kelle have recently added the title of grandparents to their nametags and they couldn't be more content. Grandparenting gives them yet another way to serve others, especially a family of young adults trying to follow the ethics John and Kelle instilled in them.

One of those significant values is faith. This is the rock that Kelle and John have stood on since day one. John depends on his faith to gain courage both in life and in business. When he took the leap to create his current wealth management practice in 1999, he did it with the confidence that faith would guide him. This same belief system is what John counts on when he's trying to follow his heart or make a decision that includes risk. Reflecting on how much good has been included in his life, John believes his faith has been the guiding light of it all.

JOHN'S FAVORITE QUOTES

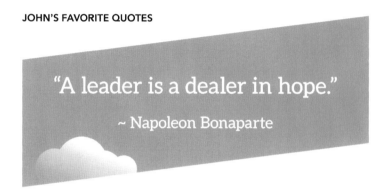

"A leader is a dealer in hope."

~ Napoleon Bonaparte

John's urge to embrace faith as a source of strength and meaningful connection to others, including those he serves on the UGM Rescue Van, was inspired by Pastor Robin Hadfield. Seeking curiosity and engagement nearly everywhere he steps, John acknowledges his desire to help others was instilled by this lifelong friend. Hadfield's friendship helped John understand that serving others, including clients, employees, and family, is an actual way of life, not just a spare time activity. John Freitag was a confidant who understood the value of meaningful conversations and passed this value to John. Freitag was also responsible for demonstrating what it means to be loyal, a value both men hold in high regard. Looking back at his adolescence, John credits his sixth-grade teacher, Mr. Gibson, for taking note of his keen leadership strength, a skill set John continues to evolve to this day. But, it was his friend Lynn who taught John to be introspective in a way that's enabled him to understand his highest purpose. John credits Lynn for helping him realize that a life of serving others requires equal time and attention, whether you're conducting business as a CEO or connecting with a man living in a windblown tent under a bridge in the middle of the night.

JOHN'S FAVORITE QUOTES

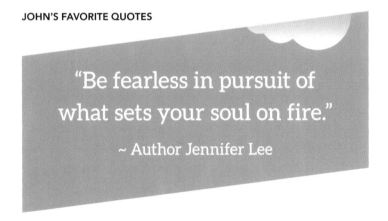

"Be fearless in pursuit of what sets your soul on fire."
~ Author Jennifer Lee

John is both grateful and humbled to know that these remarkable people have made him the man and servant leader he is today. In addition to the direction and mentorship he received from others, John believes his education has also had a significant impact on his accomplishments. His intellect and curiosity were forged during his classroom days. This knowledge base is where John's drive to expand his learning by obtaining industry-leading credentials was born. John inspires those around him, particularly members of his office team, to acquire similar education to better their career tool box. He believes all education and the experience that comes after it equals wisdom that would be difficult to obtain any other way. John has gathered plenty of knowledge outside the classroom as well. An understanding of the pace of his professional and personal growth is a balance he works to achieve every day. Since he's a forerunner, his team takes their cues from him. John knows his actions are on display whether it's as a CEO, dad, or community leader.

Another piece of sage advice John works to sustain in his life is to go into every day as if there will be no tomorrow. This reality check helps him answer the question if what is in front of him is a top priority or if there might be a better use of his time. This especially resonates when it comes to his family and friends. If connecting with someone he loves is what drives that day's agenda, John's learned to listen for that calling and it always ends with a hug.

John has confidence that people are created to be individualistic and true to who they were meant to be. He shares with others the important gift of encouraging them to seek out their own special contribution to the world. In part, this is how he leads his office team and family. By always offering his own unique attributes, he helps others find theirs.

The genesis for a lot of that good has been sourced through written goals and plans. As an external thinker, John elevates his dreams into the present day by first committing internal aspirations to paper. By intentionally speaking them aloud, John puts all his efforts in motion towards the desired outcome. This methodology has been a part of his plan book for most of his life. Much of this process of getting dreams from imagination to reality is how John helps his clients create the specific life they desire. John's *Living Fully*™ objective helps drive the balance of his life in family, business, and community.

Although John sees need everywhere he turns, the love he and Kelle share with men and women on the Union Gospel Mission Van rest well with them. As they lean over to offer a cup of hot chocolate, a sandwich and a dry pair of socks, each interaction brings a different story of loss, lack of hope, and desperation to survive. Sleet and brisk winds don't make these conversations easy but for John and Kelle, these are the people to which they're called.

At the final stop, nearing midnight, the van is nearly empty of supplies. A man comes shuffling to the back of the van desperately looking for a pair of gloves to get him through the night. Digging through the empty bins, looking under the seats, and checking the shelves to see if something had fallen out of sight, the volunteers couldn't supply the man with anything except plastic handle bags left over from the donations brought in by volunteers. The man struggled to stand in the freezing cold. Stepping close to him, John decided to do what he's always done. He removed his own gloves and placed them on someone that needed them much more than he did. John hugged the homeless man, giving him much more love than either of them realized.

Each of the inspired volunteers loaded into the van and returned to the mission to make their way home to their own warm beds, refrigerators full of food and waiting families that loved them. John and Kelle made the half hour drive to their warm and comfortable home. Halfway there, John realized his life would never be the same after this night of serving hundreds of human souls who were deeply in need of love. That night, John gave away the most love he'd ever given. When he removed his gloves to help that man get through a freezing night under a bridge, his wedding ring of 32 years went with them. Concerned and worried at first, John and Kelle later realized how much love was embedded in that band of gold. It was the same depth of love they aspire to give back as a couple to the world every day. Somehow, it was fitting.

JOHN CHRISTIANSON

"Without a sense
of caring,
there can be
no sense
of community."

~ Anthony J D'Angelo

YOUR TURN
WORKBOOK

Have you ever met someone that captured your attention immediately, to the point where you couldn't wait for the next time you'd be together? That's what *Which One Am I?* is all about. Extraordinary people stand out because they each have a unique set of qualities we admire. I believe YOU possess similar attributes that make YOU extraordinary as well.

I wrote this book to help you reflect on your own remarkable gifts. The fact is, no one moves through the world without impacting others. If you weren't here, the world would be a different place and the people you have inspired, without even knowing you were doing it, woud have been worse off for not knowing you.

Which One am I? is about identifying how you make YOUR difference in the world. Start by answering the questions in this workbook. Really think about them and see what you discover about how extraordinary you really are.

1

Name three people who bring out the best version of yourself.

Notes:

2

**Describe
yourself
at your
very
best.**

Notes:

3

As you reflect on the most important moments of your life, which five people helped make those accomplishments possible?

Notes:

4

Who are three people whose accomplishments you've influenced?

Notes:

5

What are five attributes of an extraordinary person?

Notes:

Loving
Forgiving
Kind · Committed
Positive · Faithful
Happy

EPILOGUE

JEAN SNYDER, MY MOM

(1934-2017)

> This is my mother's story. She is the influence in me
> that helps me see the extraordinary capacity in others.
> This is my family. These are the people I come from, and
> the people I honor. These are the lessons of compassion
> I work to emulate every day of my life. ~ L.S

I

A black and white sign hung at eye level above the row of kids coat hooks. PICK UP TIME IS 6:00 PM PLEASE BE ON TIME OR BE PREPARED TO PAY OUR STAFF $10 FOR EVERY 15 MINUTES YOU ARE LATE, THE DIRECTOR. It was 6:30 PM, and Anna, age two, and Mary, age three, continued to push Play-Doh through the yellow press at the purple kid-height table. Multiple attempts to reach their single mom had gone unanswered. Another thirty minutes passed. Director Jean Snyder had a tough decision to make. With four children and a devoted husband at home, adding two more for the night seemed impossible. But taking these two well-behaved Alaska Native American girls to the King County Protective Services office seemed like the least compassionate move and unthinkable. So, she left a note on the front door of the Starter School in Holly Park, Washington: *"I have taken Anna and Mary home, please call 878-4923."*

It was novel having two extra guests around the dinner table. Dinner was an hour past the normal start time. Although many questions remained, the routine of a family needed to be honored. Homework, music practice, and time with Mom and Dad around the TV ensued. Once the house calmed down, Jean began the conversation by sharing options. Dad understood and wasn't surprised by Jean's compassionate reaction. After all, she and her staff of ten cared for 100 of Seattle's most vulnerable welfare children in one of the city's toughest neighborhoods. Jean's primary mission at the Starter School was to provide a loving, peaceful environment where each child could discover their undervalued potential, get the day's best meal, and at least get a shot at a better path than the road of their parents.

The following day ended the same way. Anna and Mary's mother did not retrieve her two small daughters. The prior evening's conversation between Jean and Larry had ended with an understanding that this house of six children would be a one-night event. If their mom didn't appear, the girls would become part of the state emergency welfare care system. Once again, Jean Snyder stood at the front desk. Her only option was to drive six miles north to central Seattle and abandon these small souls to the public system. It would put their lives on an even more uncertain path. Nonetheless, it had to be done.

The traffic light at Empire Way and Kenyon Street always took forever to change. At two lanes each way and a center turn lane, Empire Way was a 45 mph north and south route many used as an alternative to Interstate 5. It was rare for motorists to travel under 50 mph. Before the traffic light was installed, the crosswalk traversing this legal speedway was a life and death roulette. A significant number of the families needed to play this dangerous game to drop off and retrieve their kids from Jean Snyder's Starter School. Every day brought the screeching of tires as moms tried to get across this major thoroughfare. With each near miss, the voice in Jean's head to somehow get the City of Seattle to install a stoplight became deafening. Even in 1978, the wheels of progress at Seattle City Hall moved at a snail's pace. Jean knew one of two options would get the attention of Ruby Chow, a recently-elected member of the King County Council for the district that included Holly Park. The determined mid-40s Jean was confident that it was just a matter of time before one of her 100 favorite children and their family would be wiped out by at least one car traveling at freeway speed.

Not following the typical path of an activist, Jean rallied her staff in the lunch room one day during the daily nap time. Every one of the ten staff agreed. The four-lane speedway was going to take a life and none of them wanted it to be one from their class. Jean distributed a draft of a flyer. The headline was easy to understand: RUBY CHOW-GET A TRAFFIC LIGHT AT THIS INTERSECTION. CALL CITY HALL 684-2489. The remaining text included a sentence about parents living in fear twice a day when crossing Empire Way. It was the final line of text that eventually kicked Ruby Chow and friends into high gear. WE WILL CONTINUE TO BLOCK TRAFFIC EVERY FRIDAY AT 4:30 PM UNTIL A PLAN IS IN PLACE TO INSTALL A TRAFFIC LIGHT AT EMPIRE WAY AND KENYON. Each staff member agreed to participate, knowing there could be consequences, but acknowledging the cost of doing nothing was far too high.

Councilwoman Chow was invited to a Friday meeting at the school. The agenda of that meeting was not disclosed except that a community forum would be present. From the sidewalk, Ruby watched as 100 children, led by a staff of ten and dozens of parents, ground Empire Way to a halt for 20 minutes. Angry commuters accepted the flyers reluctantly. Eventually, the Seattle Police were able to navigate their way to the scene. The message had been delivered. Within five days, a fast track plan was drawn, and within 90 days a traffic light was installed. Every decision at the Starter School began and ended with these 100 under-actualized children in mind. Jean saw it as her life's work to make sure that those hours within the four walls of her school created at least a small opportunity for each child to know their value and potential.

Now Jean sat at the crossroads of a decision, paused in her moment of truth by the very light she had fought to win. The light was about to change. Jean had to steer the extra-long brown and white Dodge school van either north to place the girls on an unknown path or south to beg forgiveness for her outrageous compassion. Two lives hung in the balance sitting on the tan vinyl seat behind her. She could hear her mother's voice imparting the family's favorite quote: *Do unto others as you would have them do unto you.* With a green light, Jean moved the steering wheel from left to right, turning the van to the south, toward home.

Jean's husband, Larry, was not surprised to see the side door of the van open in front of the family house. This routine continued for several years while Jean and Larry acted as guardians on behalf of the Bureau of Indian Affairs. Anna and Mary, my sisters since that first night at the dinner table, have since shared a level of love and appreciation that cannot be measured in depth or breadth. The rest of our family gained a rich understanding of the challenges faced by people who have less privilege than we do. Anna and Mary were seamlessly wrapped into our family through love. My mother's choice that day became the seed that grew into my own sense of civil responsibility.

Many lessons early in life prepared Jean for her extraordinary life. She was raised in Seattle's Georgetown neighborhood, on the northern edge of Boeing field. Her father, Arvester (A.B.), spent most of his days chasing gold in Alaska. Her mother, Frances, all five-foot of her, spent her days trying to serve and please others. She was the architect of the "Hand Up," and gave food and shelter freely. The three miniature apartments across the courtyard from the family's two-story white house often sheltered those of very limited means. Frances had a tight timeline on their days under her roof. Frances and Jean cleaned offices after hours in the nearby buildings. The funds from that work were nearly always given to benefit others. Even with an absent father, family values of a consistent work ethic and love of family had to be honored. Several lasting values passed from mom to daughter, the most important of which was no matter how tough the request: *Always try to get to yes!* This attribute showed up in almost every aspect of Jean's life from being wife, to being mom, and to running businesses.

Jean's father instilled in her another quality that two generations later is still paying dividends. *Be honest with yourself and everyone around you.* His love of this quality was rooted in humility as he had no room for being boastful at the expense of others. This also served Jean throughout her days when offered leadership posts or positions of trust. As a preschool day care director for nearly four decades, Jean had plenty of opportunities to demonstrate her early life lessons. Reluctant moms and dads would entrust Jean and staff with their most precious gift from God. Each parent was given whatever time and comforting ear was needed to experience the peace of mind that they'd made the right decision about who would care for their child.

After the transition out of the city and into Des Moines, a seaside, residential community 20 miles south of downtown Seattle, Jean's ability to gain the trust of a suburban clientele was realized. Upon learning they were expecting, families would approach her hoping to gain a coveted spot in the nursery room at Des Moines Child Care. A business family formed around Jean, made up of staff, parents, and community leaders. Frances and A.B.'s lessons of *Always try to get to yes!* and *Be honest with yourself and everyone around you* provided a path for the next generation to follow. Daughter Carol continued to take on more leadership using these same attributes, as well as earning her Early Childhood college degree. Every other family member took on roles as time permitted. When cash flow challenges arose, family members contributed to ensure Des Moines Child Care continued to function. Like many small businesses, the bookkeeper was key to managing

Jean and Carol's need to say yes to families in need. "Pay your taxes on time!" became bookkeeper Diane's rallying cry. She was Jean's financial savior for a decade. Diane was also key to negotiating with creditors, including the IRS. Each low tide brought increasing stress on Jean and a staff who were doing a job more for the love than the money. Family members continued to float Des Moines Child Care.

Jean began to rely on the only thing she knew was bigger than money. The writings of Dr. Norman Vincent Peale in his Guideposts magazine became her tool of faith. Dr. Peale's book *Power of Positive Thinking* was never far from Jean's reach. Her loving husband, Larry, all five daughters, and I began asking for divine abundance. Just days before a state revenue agency grace period expired and the business was to be forcibly shut down, a gift in the form of a larger-than-expected annual bonus came from Larry's furniture business. God delivered a miracle. Although that was not the last cash flow crisis for Jean and the nearly 100 families that counted on her extraordinary love of their children, it was the wake-up call needed to get the financial house in order. Daughter Carol expanded her role and Larry took the bus driver and maintenance duties after an accomplished four decades in home furnishings.

A new word started circulating in the school: Retirement. The business, and separately the real estate, had an excellent upside for the right buyer. Jean's biggest worry about a pending sale was not financial. Her loyal and dedicated staff had to stay intact. They too had taken on

A.B.'s mottos of dedication and honesty. Without Jean and Carol, how was this mission to continue? Both Jean and Carol agreed to stay on during a transition period not just to maintain continuity among staff but also to calm parents who recognized this changing of the guard as a significant shift in their lives too. Not one to sit still, the typical path of retirement did not agree with Jean. After settling in to a 55+ housing community, traveling to places old people are supposed to visit and getting the new yard just right, it was time to find another purpose.

II

My mom, Jean Snyder, was a living example of how much comes back to you when you live a life of generosity and care for others. The ripple effect of her selfless love is enormous. Nothing could have been clearer proof of this dynamic than the devotion our family showed Jean as she slipped into dementia.

My dad took on every task, including cooking (to prevent stove fires and stop refrigerated items from ending up in the pantry). He tended to Jean's every need, monitored her every movement. Frighteningly, before we knew just how advanced the dementia had become, Jean disappeared from the family home twice – each time Larry turned his back for only a moment and she was gone, setting off frantic, hours-long searches. It became clear to Larry that he could not protect Jean on his own. He called a Sunday family dinner meeting. His agenda was finding a solution to get the proper care for Jean and to find it as soon as possible. The pool of resources among the children in the family was about to become valuable. First-born daughter, Kathy, brought ambition and generosity. Carol, the daughter who spent most of her life as Jean's business partner, was the one who could still communicate with Jean. I became the problem solver and eternal optimist. Annie, with her heart of gold invested every spare hour at Jean's side, giving Dad a respite, if only 30 minutes to grab a cup of coffee and read the paper without the constant supervision of Jean's movements and whereabouts. Spouses of each family member stood by and supported everything, all the time.

Larry and Jean's life was about to take a very different path from the one they'd known during their almost 70 years together. Other than a few business trips and Jean's time in the rehab center after her double knee replacement, Jean and Larry had spent very few evenings apart.

Though it was not an easy transition – it was harrowing at times, to be sure – Jean finally found a place at the Spring Ridge memory care facility in Tacoma. All of us in the family were grateful for the care and safety Spring Ridge provided, especially Na'ti, a tall, strong, Samoan transplant who took a specific interest in making sure Jean's needs were acknowledged. Jean went through many months of upheaval and struggle adjusting to other facilities before Spring Ridge helped her settle in her final months.

Part of that settling-in process required that the family stay away for a time so the staff could observe Jean, learn her patterns and needs free of our input or influence. Larry was able to sustain not seeing Jean for five days before he needed to see the woman he'd been with for nearly 70 years. His 60-minute round trip drive to and from Tacoma, in addition to the many hours trying to keep his mind occupied with positive thoughts, gave him ample time to reflect on their amazing life together. These beautiful thoughts included the day he met a warm-hearted 14-year-old girl when she visited his uncle's corner gas station looking for air to put in her bicycle tire. Another was falling in love through the mail while he was at war in Korea. For, as weak as Jean's ability to remember her extraordinary past had become, Larry's mind was 180 degrees the opposite. His solitude enabled him to reflect on their early courtship; best times shared with other couples; how he'd taught Jean to fish; and how, ultimately, he'd taken his girl across the border to elope. He reminisced about their days of struggle in business. With both husband and wife leading separate businesses, the peaks and valleys of entrepreneurship presented plenty of challenges. Larry knew the strength and commitment of the husband/wife partnership allowed them to weather their respective storms. A thousand other satisfying, incredibly vivid, lifetime memories filled his mind. If this was to be the final curtain for Jean's life, Larry continued to acknowledge that he could not have been partnered in a better union. In times of greater clarity, Jean would share gratitude for her kind, loving, and faithful husband. Jean also spent at least part of each day giving thanks to Larry for the three children they created together and the final two children that came into the family because he understood her limitless need to live in the deepest form of compassion. She would regularly remind him how much pride she had for each one of her kids. Even as Jean's mind slipped into dementia, her love for Larry and her family prevailed.

III

"For where your treasure is, there your heart will be also."

~ Matthew 6:21

The long struggle of watching a most caring, selfless, beautiful woman's progress through the stages of an irreversible cognitive disease was heartbreaking and terribly sad. Even though Jean couldn't manage her own thoughts and memories, each family member sat at her side reminding her of the valuable role she'd played in getting her kids ready for life. Because the future was so cloudy, nearly every bedside talk focused on the best times from the past. Jean wasn't just an outstanding mom to her own children and the hundreds of brave parents who left their kids in her care, she was also the mom most moms wanted to be. Her good-natured smile, consistent humming, and gratitude for the help of her staff was noticed by all. Even when circumstances should have elicited a negative response, those closest to Jean always saw her looking at the bright side of any problem.

Eventually, with Jean's lack of mobility, limited verbal responses, and inability to take in solid foods, the word *hospice* was presented to Larry in a morning conversation with Na'ti. Larry, Annie, Carol, Kathy and I joined at Jean's bedside. A steady stream of grandchildren began to visit, knowing this might be their final opportunity to express their love for an influence in their lives that will live on forever. Jean often expressed her pleasure in seeing the next generation take on the values and attributes of the family of which she was so proud.

Even though they had dozens of other residents under their care, Na'ti and other members of the Spring Ridge care team visited every 10-15 minutes instead of the normal hourly visit. Na'ti began openly sharing her fondness for Jean as her eyes became misty. She also reiterated how she'd never seen an entire family care so much. Each time

Na'ti would leave the room, she'd let Larry know she could be found just around the corner if he needed her. With all six family members sharing a 12x12 space nearly 48 hours in a row, the Spring Ridge staff made sure everyone was able to find a place to rest. Realizing the most sacred quality of these final moments, each family member shared their most important family memories with Jean. Larry expressed his deep appreciation for being husband to the greatest wife and mother of his children. He acknowledged her love of life, positive impact on everyone who had the honor of knowing her, and how she showed compassion daily.

In the closing hours of Jean's extraordinary life, two more visitors waited in the hall outside Jean's tiny room. With tears running down their cheeks, Anna and Mary turned the corner to see Jean for the final time. The two lives that could have turned out so differently were the two final members of the family to gather around Jean in her last moments.

JEAN SNYDER

LARRY AND JEAN SNYDER

ACKNOWLEDGMENTS

One of the most important lessons I took from writing this book was learning that right below the surface of most people exists a desire to contribute at a higher level. Some have the ability to give money, others a talent or skillset, but I believe the commodity that most wish they had more of is time. Three of the four us on this writing team said goodbye to our mothers recently. What each of us would give for another year, week or day to show them the gifts they contributed to our lives. This book is about honor. When we look back at the most influential people in our lives, a bit of every decision we make was formed by a lesson, a kind word, some corrective feedback, or even a dose of tough love. And how we live, whether we are conscious of it or not, honors those lessons, those formative moments and the people who gave them.

No one writes a book alone. The contributors to this project are a collective set of professional, creative, loyal and fun human beings whom I wish to honor for looking to present the world with a written body of work in its best form. Having a publisher, friend, and confidant in Ethan Yarbrough provided me with confidence, peace of mind, and shared values of telling a story that makes the reader ask more questions. My absolute gratitude for the design, look, and feel of this book rests with Sonja Gerard who takes my abstract thoughts and somehow creates exactly what

I was thinking in a beautiful graphic expression. Knowing that editor Catherine Lenox is crystal clear on the intent of my message means that every correction and rewrite will be much better than I could have ever done it myself. All 12 extraordinary people profiled in this book allowed me and you a picture window view into their thoughts on very personal and impactful subjects. There aren't enough words to recognize them for their trust, so I'll do what my extraordinary mother taught me and say, *Thank You*. To my partner Jill, mother of our terrific daughter, Daniela: you afforded me the countless hours of writing time and the sharing of our family budget to produce this book; I am so thankful. Little of this story would have any real value if it wasn't for my late mother, Jean, my father, Larry, my sisters Kathy, Carol, Annie, and my foster sisters Mary and Anna. Without them all I wouldn't understand the meaning of unconditional love, forgiveness, or what it means to be a family that's all in for each other. I'm overjoyed that Margaret Larson said yes to penning the foreword. She has been a constant inspiration for me and I'm quite grateful for our friendship. Finally, to that little girl on a makeshift soccer field in West Africa, your four words created a movement. Many people, myself included, will soon recognize living from the inside out makes it a lot easier to answer the question, Which One Am I?

ABOUT THE TEAM

LARRY J. SNYDER
Author | Speaker

Larry has spent most of his life either listening to or telling stories. With a 31-flavor past, Larry has settled into a rhythm of life that includes helping domestic and international causes with philanthropy and fundraising support. His own efforts are inspired by the examples he witnesses in others. *Which One am I? 12 Extraordinary People, Like You!* is Larry's attempt to share the stories of a dozen human beings who have inspired him by impacting the world in a lasting and meaningful way. His gratitude extends to the members of the team that made this book a reality. Each of the team members listed here is extraordinary in their contribution to this book and to the world.

CATHERINE LENOX
Editor

Owner and Founder of Write Contact, author Catherine Lenox ghostwrites creative non-fiction books, articles, and blogs. A former radio news reporter and writer/editor for numerous publications, she enjoys helping others tell their stories. Raised by philanthropic, community-minded parents, she attended a Quaker high school where she learned the importance of social responsibility, love and community. She joined the *Which One Am I?* creative team because the book resonates with her own desire to impact the world in a meaningful way.

ETHAN YARBROUGH
Publisher

Ethan Yarbrough is a content, communication and editorial strategist by trade and a book publisher by passion. He is the founder and creative lead at Iron Twine Press where he indulges in the deep satisfaction of helping authors move their books from idea to reality. The knowledge and inspiration he gains from each new project enrich his life immeasurably.

TEAM'S MOTTO

To balance freaking out with figuring it out.

SONJA GERARD
Book Designer

"Okay, I'll make it fit and add some visuals," as I smile. I really enjoyed working on this book with the best team ever! We were very cognizant that the profiles in this book were not in any significant order (other than Mother Jean). They are equally important. I learned a lot from every one of these profiled individuals, truly. I love my family, my friends, my dog (if I had one), helping and creating. Thank you Larry for this wonderful opportunity!

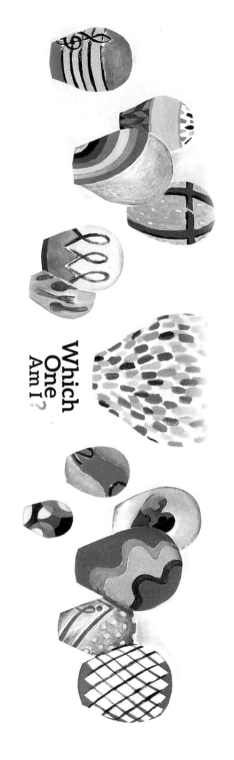

Which
One
Am I ?